Dedication

To my wife Pat, who encouraged me, read my work, and provided ideas and comments. Married less than a year and with limited resources, she encouraged me to maintain an emergency fund to fly to New York for trips to my home. After Mom died, Dad continued to live in the neighborhood. I visited Dad three to five times a year; Pat stayed behind several times. Much of the inspiration for *Growing Up in New York's Italian South Village* occurred during Dad's last years.

Without Pat's love there would have been fewer visits. Reality would have mirrored the scene from Frank Capra's *It's a Wonderful Life*, where Clarence shows George Bailey what would happen if he had never existed.

Without Pat's love, this book would not have existed.

Grazie, ti amo,
Tony

Growing Up in New York's Italian South Village

Tony Vivolo

BOOK PUBLISHERS NETWORK

Book Publishers Network
P.O. Box 2256
Bothell • WA • 98041
PH • 425-483-3040
www.bookpublishersnetwork.com

10 9 8 7 6 5 4 3 2 1
Printed in the United States of America

LCCN   2010910777
ISBN10 1-935359-47-9
ISBN13 978-1-935359-47-0

The photo used on the front cover of the book; courtesy of the Shrine of Saint Anthony of Padua.

The photo of 120 Sullivan Street used on the back cover of the book and also within the text together with the photo of 107 Sullivan Street, courtesy of the NYC Municipal Archives.

The map provided of the South Village used in the text, courtesy of the Greenwich Village Society for Historical Preservation.

Editor: Julie Scandora
Cover Designer: Laura Zugzda
Typographer: Stephanie Martindale

A portion of the proceeds of every book sold will be donated to the Greenwich Village Society for Historical Preservation and their efforts to preserve the South Village, in honor of Rosemary (Rosso) Muzio, D'avanzo.

Contents

Acknowledgments

I would like to thank the following people who provided invaluable assistance on making this book a reality: Sheryn Hara, Julie Scandora, Laura Zugzda, and Stephanie Martindale. Grazie to Vince Muscolo and Maria Franzese for the Italian translations. To our children a special thanks for listening, reading, and providing support over the years.

Introduction

Dad lived his entire life in a ten-block area of lower Manhattan, born on Grand Street, moving two blocks to 57 Thompson Street with his parents and sister, and finally going two additional blocks to 120 Sullivan Street after marrying Mom. Retracing his life's journey from birth to death consists of fifteen minutes of walking and eighty-five years of living. Dad lived in the same five-story walk-up for almost fifty-five years, the first forty-two with my mother the last thirteen by himself. Life in New York City was never easy. Change always meant risk. Dad, not being a risk taker, never considered leaving the familiar—the city, his four rooms, and their memories. The neighborhood was his life. He found smiles, laughter, and loving memories in every step of his daily walk, completely content in these few blocks. The Italian neighborhood of the South Village sheltered its inhabitants from the outside world, beckoning through radio, television, Hollywood, and magazines. Only a bold few asked, "What's out there?" The neighborhood replied, "You will never have it as good as it is here, believe me. And what about the family that loves you?" The neighborhood was Dad's "secret of life." His needs met, he never looked elsewhere.

I was his only son, living three thousand miles away in Seattle with my wife and three children. After Mom's death, I kept current on his well-being through cousins, the telephone, and several visits a year. On every visit, we went to dinner at the same neighborhood restaurant, Porto Bello on Thompson Street. Dad was comfortable eating out in this restaurant and visited it only when I was home. Sometimes we ate at his tiny kitchen table with a dark green Formica tabletop and three chairs in a room so small it was necessary to move a chair to access the walk-in pantry. Porto Bello became an extension of his apartment, possessing a special gift of turning strangers into friends.

Dad and I walked, holding hands through the familiar streets of our childhoods. We walked past Saint Anthony's, the church we attended with family and friends living in the four- and five-story brick tenements above the storefronts, glancing at the stores and apartment windows, remaining silent, smiling, seeing and hearing the ghosts of the past who had occupied these buildings forty and sixty years ago. The concrete sidewalks, now cracked and spalled from old age, supported our footsteps now as they had our running and jumping in years past. The trees, originally as high as the "No Parking" sign when planted forty years ago, now towered fifty feet high, adding green in spring to the black and gray landscape.

Porto Bello was home to Dad, as if he were in his own kitchen, a feat not accomplished by any of the aunts and cousins. In every Italian family, the cook reigns supreme, recipes never completely shared or changed to accommodate anyone. If you demanded, "No cheese!" you still got cheese, "No sauce!" you still got sauce. Why ask? Would you ask Michelangelo to change David?

Al was the maitre d', a title he deservingly held for years. If Dad asked for anything or wanted something deleted, Al always respected and catered to his needs. In the comfort of Al's care, our meals extended into discussions and reminiscences. On a quiet night, we would linger for hours. At one of our last dinners when the cancer was starting to take its toll, he surprised me by sharing stories of my grandfather and his family. Dad never told intimate stories of family members or friends, speaking only when necessary, then succinctly and sparingly, with little emotion and no humor. Dad mentioned my grandfather's brother Donato, who accompanied my grandfather, together leaving Italy and arriving at Ellis Island. Having lived with my grandfather for twenty years, I had never heard Donato's name spoken. Dad told stories of relatives in Italy and those in the neighborhood, people previously unknown to me. I recognized the importance of this discussion, beginning to write on napkins and waiter's order books that Al provided.

After my father's death, I met with three remaining cousins, attempting with my notes and their input to develop a family tree. Despite our efforts, a family tree never took root, only a family bush, low growing, not worthy of a Latin horticultural name. Glancing at the few branches and boxes together with names and dates, faces, voices, and memories consumed me. The name of Elena "Helen" Greco leaped from the small box in "front page headlines." Helen was the "Head Aunt," ruling the family with love and respect for over five generations. How could we imprison Helen in a two-inch-by-one-inch box on a piece of paper when in real life keeping her out of any place a family member lived or worked in all of New York State was an impossibility.

In order to write and share your thoughts, you must know who you are. Thanks to my upbringing in this most special of neighborhoods, I know. Approaching my sixty-seventh year, my views on life's issues may change, but I remain the product of my roots. There is consistency in my thoughts and actions as a result. Life's experiences together with individuals I met nourished the roots creating my foundation. Family and neighborhood provided the soil and water, nourishing the seeds of childhood.

I decided to capture the family and neighborhood, their respect of others, joy of life, belief in the future, and unique senses of humor. The ability to laugh at one's self has always distinguished those who feel comfortable in the knowledge of who and what they are. I want to pass on to my family stories that bring life to those names in the family tree, along with the special neighborhood of which I was a part. May these stories nourish my children and generations beyond, those who grew up in Italian neighborhoods, and those who look to capture a bit of what I experienced in their own community. The future will continue to connect us by birth, marriage, and death, as it has in the past. May the family, *la famiglia*, the neighborhood, and those who contributed to who we became, never be forgotten.

Finding myself in the unplanned role of family historian, I decided to take classes to learn first how to type, then to write. I read and shared my writing with family and friends. I read Mary Pipher's *Writing to Change the World*, which helped me understand my responsibility. She says:

> A writer's job is to tell stories that connect readers to all the people of the earth, to show these people as the complicated human beings they really are, with histories, families, emotions, and legitimate needs.

As New York City's Italian South Village, the neighborhood I knew, continues to change and is in danger of disappearing, may this book allow me to complete my job as a writer and connect my family and neighborhood to you. May they continue to live in your minds and hearts.

Let us begin our journey, bringing family, friends, and the Sullivan Street of the 1950s to life. As you read this book, may a scene enter your mind; may a sound be heard, an aroma sensed, and a feeling stirred; may a bond connect you with the people you meet that will last forever.

120 Sullivan Street

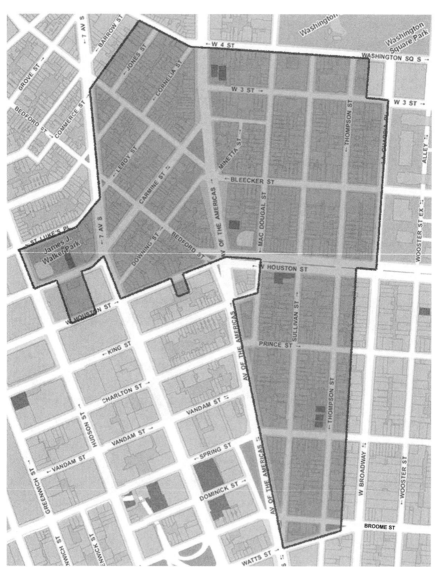

Map of the South Village Proposed Historical District

The Neighborhood

The neighborhood of my early world was my parent's only world. Growing up in the early 1950s, all my wants, needs, and love were met in a ten-block area of Manhattan, the Italian South Village. The neighborhood centered around Sullivan and Thompson Streets, from Grand Street on the south to Bleecker Street on the north. These streets were our *piazzas*.

Street-level stores and four- and five-story walk-up brick tenements provided homes for immigrants and first-generation Italians. Saint Anthony's and Our Lady of Pompeii Churches provided hope, guidance, and a place where the people felt comfortable. Pushcarts lined Sullivan Street. Fords, Chevrolets, and Studebakers parked in front of tenements, and black Buicks and Cadillac sedans in front of bars, cafes, and social clubs. The pushcarts congregated on Houston Street adjacent to Saint Anthony's Church and on Bleecker Street opposite Our Lady of Pompeii. Pushcart vendors sold vegetables, fruit, flowers, clothing, towels, utensils, raw clams, plastic handbags, and plastic medals of Saint Anthony, the Blessed Virgin, and Saint Christopher. At 7 p.m., the pushcarts disappeared. At seven the next morning, they reappeared, their contents changed. Children on steel, ball bearing roller skates cruised the sidewalks; older siblings played kick the can and baseball in the street.

There were few secrets. Everybody knew each other, their families, and their history. People hugged and kissed in the street, yelled and shook their fists, discussed intimate issues, sharing their stories and dreams on the sidewalks and stoops. The doors of tenement apartments were always open. Everyone heard everyone else's business and smelled that night's dinner menu. Most neighborhood residents had little or no education or money. The few items they had were humble. Sharing everything came easy to those who had an abundance of respect for others, belief in family, and hope for the future; these things mattered more than material possessions. The neighborhood was a large extended family, and as in every family, there is always good and bad.

The neighborhood, although poor, exuded a richness in its sounds and smells. The brick tenements lining both sides of the street amplified the noises, bringing the place alive throughout the day. The rumble of the subway, sirens, screech of brakes, and clash of garbage trucks at times drowned out the shouts of the kids playing stickball in the street and the persuasive calls of the pushcart vendors. Booming messages delivered from tenement windows to recipients on Sullivan Street pierced the background noise. Shouting within tenement apartments filled hallways, everyone loudly responding simultaneously, competing for recognition, since listening was a skill few if any possessed.

There were five grocery stores in a two-block area, from Virginia's next to Saint Anthony's Church on Sullivan and Houston Streets to Carmine's at the corner of Spring and Sullivan Streets. Virginia made cold and hot sandwiches to order. At lunchtime, the chef stood working in her kitchen at the back of the store, afterwards returning to the counter. Entering Virginia's, strangers stood motionless, their noses suggesting they had made a mistake. The film of white mold on the hanging prosciutto, pancetta, dried sausage, salami, and the sharp smells of Provolone and Locatelli cheeses assaulted the senses of non-Italians, but these fragrances delighted neighborhood residents, bringing to each memories of past Sundays and holiday meals. What set Virginia's apart from other neighborhood grocery stores was her unique sandwich menu—the perfume of sautéed veal and sweet peppers excited the senses, an aroma that fifty years later persists in my memory.

At four o'clock every afternoon, the smell of garlic cooking in olive oil escaped through restaurants' exhaust fans, floated through the neighborhood, and mingled with that of yeast, dough, oregano, and tomato sauce from Arturo's, Port Alba, and the Napoli pizzerias. The zephyr of fragrance, entwined with the essence of that night's dinners escaping the windows and doors of tenement apartments, joined to become the neighborhood's evening trade wind. From the evening's closing of the restaurants to the morning's opening of the grocery stores, four bakeries emitted the sweet perfume of baking bread from coal-fired ovens.

The neighborhood became our garden despite concrete, brick, or cobblestones covering nearly every square inch of earth. It nurtured its mature plants and seedlings, alike, cast by the winds of chance, now deeply rooted in its fertile soil. The plants grew and sprouted seeds, bearing fruit and staying firmly rooted to Sullivan Street, never leaving except in a coffin or the back of a police car.

The Italian South Village was self-contained. The grocery stores, restaurants, cafés, bars, bakeries, candy stores, chicken markets, bookies, butcher shops, cheese stores, pork stores, fish markets, vegetable stores, social clubs, pool parlors, undertaker parlors, and two churches addressed the needs of the neighborhood. Sullivan Street fed us, nurtured us, baptized us, married us, and eventually buried us.

The grocery stores and cafés were extensions of the tenement apartments, places to hang out, socialize, conduct business, the Starbucks of yesteryear, devoid of corporate plans but rich in intimacy and character. A store that was the heart and soul of my world and a part of everyone's family on Sullivan Street was Willie "The Cap's" store.

Church of Our Lady
of Pompeii

Saint Anthony's School

Saint Anthony's Church

Willie "The Cap's" Store

Outside appearances mattered little in this, one of the most important of Sullivan Street's memories. The window bore only the address "109" in peeling gold plate. Turned wooden supports, dark green and covering seventy years of previous coats of paint, surrounded the windows. Painters on Sullivan Street believed sanding or scraping before painting was not a necessity; applying another thick layer of enamel, thereby preserving forever chips, drips, and gashes that served as reminders of time past, like the annual rings of trees.

Three-foot high, cast-iron gates on each side of the entrance provided a history similar to that of the wood window supports, except the paint color was black. The gate to the left of the door had a chain with hook, preventing access to the concrete steps leading down to the side alley of the tenement. To the right of the entrance door, padlocked, diamond-plate steel cellar doors, flush with the sidewalk, provided access to the cellar stairs, the grocery store's storage area. Never painted, the doors showed rust over much of the steel, except for portions that completely disappeared where the metal had corroded.

Steel mesh, rusted in places, protected the window on the top half of the entrance door. Pushing it open, the first thing you noticed was the floor. You naturally looked downward since the door, improperly hung, required effort to open. The wood plank floor boards, never finished or sanded, each had its own characteristic pattern of wear and degree of warp. The nails fastening the planks displayed only rusted cores, the heads worn off years ago. Portions of the floor experienced significant wear, resulting in boards higher or lower than ones adjacent to them. The floor in front of the counter showed the greatest wear, dipping considerably from years of customers ordering, paying for purchases, and passing the time. Elsewhere, square pieces of worn tin nailed to the floor marked abandoned penetrations made for piping, electrical, or other purposes.

The floor undulations resulted in color variation under natural and artificial light. Eight sixty-watt bulbs created the latter, housed in white metal shades, suspended by brown, braided, fabric-covered cords from the ten-foot high ceiling. The decorative tin ceiling, like the floor, had received its original—and only—coat of paint over seventy years ago. The ceiling's original color was not white like the few small pockets and patches of wall above the shelves but light tan, explaining why color and rust blended in faintly lit areas.

There were no bare walls. Rough milled wood shelving, edged with a smooth finishing strip, covered the walls from the floor to a height of eight feet. The shelving, like the floor, had last seen an oil or varnish finish decades before. Adjacent to the entrance door was a doorway, leading to a narrow room containing a small window, covered with hardware cloth. Painted shut for years, the window looked out into the gray tenement airshaft. A mop sink was mounted directly below the window. Adjacent to the sink, a curtain-covered doorway led to a porcelain toilet. A wall-mounted metal tank, framed in wood, four feet above the toilet, contained the water used for its flush. Pulling the wooden handle attached to the chain activated the rush of water.

A cast-bronze cash register sat behind the counter. A slab of white marble served as the till cover. The register operated by a series of gears and springs. Small metal plates with painted numbers popped up in the window above the register, displaying the transaction amounts. A bell rang when the till drawer was opened. The drawer contained a wooden tray with dividers for several denominations of coins together with paper currency. Leaning over, peering into the drawer behind the dividers, you could see rolls of yellowed paper tied with string. A small piece of paper directly under the string in faded black ink identified the owners of the delinquent bills. Names of neighborhood families and dates were arranged chronologically, starting with "May 12, 1906," "December 23, 1918," "November 13, 1929." Dates and names continued until the mid 1930s. These IOUs belonged to Willie "The Cap's" father, the store's original proprietor. Willie's father came to America in the early 1880s from northern Italy outside Genoa, working as a laborer digging the subway, digging pipe trenches, digging ditches to earn enough money to open this grocery store. Willie's father and mother worked in the store, from 5 a.m. until 7 p.m., six days a week, the store their business, the neighborhood, their family. Willie, after finishing grade school, worked alongside his parents.

Each grocery store in the neighborhood catered to the different Provincial Italian dialects of neighborhood residents. Willie "The Cap's" father spoke the unique Genovese dialect, providing a place where people felt comfortable and could communicate and extending credit when banks would not. This little grocery store became the extended family for my grandparents, parents, and my generation as well.

No one used Willie "The Cap's" last name. In our neighborhood, only nicknames mattered: Bobby "Chicken Market," Jo Jo "Clams," Diane "The Bread," Bobby "Dogs," Mikie "Smash," Johnny "Eyes," Anthony "Pinhead," Frankie "Hot Dogs," "Mopey" Phil, and Mike "Whata yah say?" who greeted people with his nickname. Everyone in the neighborhood had a nickname; only strangers or cops used last names.

Willie "The Cap," got his nickname from a World War II, navy knit cap he rarely took off, some say due to a receding hairline. Willie was a most important part of neighborhood life, becoming our historian, philosopher, and sociologist, cherishing his role and his customers. The grocery store was a testimonial and memorial to his father, together with the hundreds upon hundreds of families who came before us. Willie ruled his domain creating harmony, understanding, and maintaining an ambiance consistent since the early 1900s. He always had time to visit, inquire about family, discuss politics, religion, or sports, and gossip. He gave us a spot to stay warm in winter, place a bet with the resident bookmaker, and share a laugh. He created more than a grocery store, open six days a week from six until seven, and it kept Willie working into his mid seventies; his customers became his extended family.

At the street window stood a series of unpainted wooden shelves, installed at an angle intended for displaying vegetables and fruit to the passing public. Such food never occupied those shelves; instead, only an unusual mechanical device to retrieve items on shelves to high to reach by hand lay across one. The upper shelves contained those items Willie termed "non-movers." A non-mover to Willie meant something not requested for a year or, maybe, a decade or two. Shelves above five feet were only accessible by "The Cap" through this mechanical gripping device, consisting of two metal rods with handles, mounted on a six-foot broomstick. The handles on each side of the broomstick opened and closed two steel, four-inch, semicircular jaws, attached by springs to the steel rods that fit over items as large as a twenty-eight-ounce can of whole tomatoes. The jaws, covered with ribbed rubber sleeves, applied pressure and securely held the smooth face of cans stored high above.

In awe, I'd watch Willie "The Cap", five foot four and weighing no more than 130 pounds, raise the gripper in his right hand, clutch a can of tomatoes eight feet above the floor, move the can laterally from the shelf, then release the jaws to drop the twenty-eight-ounce can effortlessly into his left hand. "The Cap" made baseball's Willie May's famous basket catches in the Polo Grounds look like child's play.

"Willie, why don't you use the ladder?"

"I'm afraid of heights. If I ever saw all the dust on the top shelves I'd feel guilty, hearing my mother tell me to clean the shelves. I could get a heart attack cleaning the shelves. Now you wouldn't want that to happen to a nice guy like me, do you? You won't have anyone to help you pick your winners at the track." With a twinkle in his blue eyes, he'd end, saying, "What you don't know won't hurt you."

The podium for the store's conductor was the area around the cash register. In front of the podium, a four-and-a-half-foot high white refrigerated case displayed Italian cold cuts, imported cheeses, and buckets of fresh mozzarella. Directly to the right was Willie's pride and joy, the stainless steel meat-slicing machine with a twelve-inch circular blade.

Mounted on a portion of the counter, lower than the display case, the machine provided the customer with an unobstructed view of "The Cap" performing intricate movements, creating his unique work of sandwich art, while insuring the thickness of each slice was as desired. The cutting machine turned on, the lights dimmed, and the whine of the motor increased in pitch, filling the store and drowning out the radio. Willie spent much of his day at the machine, slicing cold cuts, bantering with his customers, raising his two-foot long knife, slicing bread, onions, pickles, tomatoes, soft and hard cheeses. Willie "The Cap," the maestro of sandwiches, directed the luncheon concerto. He played to his season ticket holders six days a week, fifty-two weeks a year, except religious holidays.

Willie's radio was always on, loud enough to hear the music but not loud enough to hear the announcer, except during the World Series or Kentucky Derby. Willie sang along with all the songs, whether knowing the words or not, a smiling soprano with a twinkle in his blue eyes.

On rare occasions, Willie raised his voice, demanding silence. Everything stopped. You knew only breathing was acceptable, then only in silence. Willie, in white apron and blue-checkered shirt, would raise his baton, tilt his head with its sparse gray hair, focus his angelic blue eyes to the tan rust tin ceiling as the radio played Domenico Modugno singing "Nel Blu Dipinto Di Blu (Volare)." "Volare" in the 1950s was the first popular song on an American radio station completely in Italian. Out of respect, Willie expected silence until the song was over, although singing along was OK, but talking prohibited much like our national anthem.

My friends and I grew up playing in the street always spending our lunch money, if we had any, at "Cap's." You never ordered lunch you debated it. Whatever you ordered Willie challenged you. "Why so big a sandwich?" "Why are you mixing mustard with mayo?" "Why do you need a devil dog?" "Why are you having soda and not milk?" "Does your mother know you're not in school?" "Why?" Willie at times had us wash our hands before giving us our sandwiches. Willie challenged adult's purchases in a similar manner, equal treatment for all.

The "gang," as Willie called all sixteen of us, ages eight through twelve, entered for lunch. There was a mad rush to the counter to see who would be first in line. After shoves, kicks, and elbows, I made it to the middle of the line. It was cold outside with a strong wind blowing off the Hudson. We had played two-hand touch football on the frosted asphalt street since eight that morning. I reached into the right front pocket of my torn jeans to get my lunch money. It was gone! After frantically searching every pocket, I slowly moved out of line, sitting on a milk crate, deciding to keep warm while my teammates consumed lunches next to me. My stomach loudly voiced its displeasure.

Willie, after making everyone's sandwiches, looked over.

"Where's your lunch?"

"I'm not hungry; I had a big breakfast."

Wordlessly he walked over to the rear wall to the screened wooden breadboxes, reached in, and took out a piece of Italian bread. Walking over to the slicing machine and picking up the end of salami, he turned on the machine, cutting two slices. Willie put the meat into the Italian bread he had sliced, spread some mustard on it, and presented it to me.

"The bread was stale. I was going to throw it out anyway. It's not worth more than a nickel. Pay me when you can."

I wonder how many times since 1906 Willie's dad and Willie said, "Pay me when you can."

Willie "The Cap"
and me

109 and 107 Sullivan Street

Different Voices

Listening, to people speak.
Understanding, so little.

Walking, head down,
On unfamiliar streets.

Turning from eye contact,
Avoiding being spoken to.

Encountering rejection,
Seeking acceptance.

Finding understanding,
Receiving respect,

In a grocery store.

My Mother's Parents

Today, children grow up, rarely knowing both sets of grandparents. The mobility and affluence of society limits visits to holidays and important family occasions, the only time children spend with these special people. During these short-term visits, everyone is on his or her best or worst behavior, with true bonding difficult to achieve in an artificially structured environment. I was lucky growing up with both sets of grandparents. Everyday became a holiday, and their time with me a gift I savored then and still cherish today.

Mom's parents came from a rural area outside Genoa in northern Italy. Dad's parents were from Naples in southern Italy. The dialects differed enough that both sets of grandparents had difficulty communicating with each other. They often resorted to facial expressions or hand signals, the spoken word carefully selected when used and then only at the appropriate moment. For me, many times they would search for words, and if not found, direct smiles, hugs, and kisses to me much like run-on sentences.

We lived in a five-story tenement at 120 Sullivan Street. Dad's parents lived with us in a two-bedroom, four-room apartment on the top floor. Mom's parents lived with Aunt Mamie in a one-bedroom, three-room apartment three stories below. Dad's sister Rosie, her husband, Jimmy, and children, Jamsie, Rosemary, and Anthony, lived in the apartment directly beneath us on the fourth floor. As a child, I always had somebody nearby to love and someone to love me, somebody to get in trouble with and someone to be forgiven by.

The brick tenement, built in the late 1920s to house the arriving immigrants, was one of the newer buildings on the block. A single stairway, framed in structural steel with wide granite steps, their once square edges now curved and worn by the thousands of trips up and down, gave access to the five stories of apartments. Hallways were laid with one-inch green, gray, and white hexagonal tiles. The gray and white tiles became home plate and bases for games of hallway slap-ball and off-the-wall, a place for children to play, safely away from traffic, within hearing and yelling distance. Two windows on each landing opened to an airshaft shared with the adjacent building. Everything in a tenement was shared. The airshaft provided air for ventilation and light to the hallway. The airshaft also served as a place to dry clothes.

Each floor contained a dumbwaiter, or chute, for sending garbage from the hallway directly to the basement. The space originally had housed a toilet, shared by all five apartments on the floor. Remodeled apartments with bathrooms and bathtubs provided the space for the dumbwaiter. A coal furnace in the basement supplied heat and hot water through a system of pipes and radiators. At the time of the building's construction, the need for electricity was limited. Our apartment had a fuse box with two fifteen-amp circuits. Lights, radio, and refrigerator were OK, but lights, radio, refrigerator, and toaster not OK.

My mother's parents, Bartolomeo and Dominica DeVincenzi, were the building superintendents. Together with the help of family, they held the job and rent-free apartment that came with it for over twenty years, until both were in their mid seventies.

My grandfather, Nonno, stoked the coal furnace seven days a week, fifty-two weeks a year. To practice his skills, he shoveled garbage from the dumbwaiter shaft into thirty-gallon metal cans, carrying the cans up steep concrete cellar steps to Sullivan Street for pickup by the Department of Sanitation. Once the cans were empty, he returned them to the basement, cleaning and rearranging them for the new nightly deposits.

Nonno performed minor repairs to the building, painting apartments, hallways, and fire escapes on a rotating schedule. When the work exceeded my grandfather's physical ability, Aunt Mamie notified Helen, the Head Aunt. On weekends and holidays, all my uncles and aunts arrived, assisting with major repairs, painting, and working with my *nonno*. My grandparents' oldest son, Albert, lived in Staten Island, had three children, and worked in the city. Uncle Albert worked five and a half or six days a week, often spending his Saturday afternoons or Sundays helping my grandfather. My grandmother Nonna and her two youngest daughters, Mom and Aunt Mamie, cleaned the windows, floors, stairways, and steps, swept the sidewalk in front of the building, and helped with all the chores.

In 1906, Bartolomeo had left Valleti, a village in the mountains above Genoa. The family worked on farms, clearing land, raising vegetables, chickens, sheep, and goats. A meager supply of food rewarded them for their hard work. My grandfather left the security of his village with a few liras in his pocket, no job skills, and no ability to read or write English or Italian. He left his twenty-six-year-old wife with two daughters and two sons in Italy to fend for themselves until he could earn enough money to send for them. They joined him seven years later.

Nonno took work as a day laborer. A proud hard man, he refused any charitable gifts, always making do with what he had, putting up with pain, and not going to the doctor because "*Costa troppo* (it costs too much)." Nonno spent seven years alone in a strange land, taking any job, working twelve-hour days, saving every dollar for his family. He accomplished what was necessary for his dream to become reality. Only my grandfather knew what those years were like, never discussing this with anyone.

My grandparents continued to live in New York City exactly as they had lived in Valetti, their village in Italy. They planted a garden on the fire escape—tomatoes, lettuce, parsley, basil, onions, rosemary, and garlic—in clay pots and tin cans. The bounty from the garden always found its way into the daily meals. Together my grandparents proudly described in Italian which seasoning component of the salad or *primo* or *secondo* came from their garden. Thank God, there was never a fire in any of the apartments in 120 Sullivan Street. The fire escapes stacked with clay and tin pots and wooden planting boxes would have made evacuation difficult if not impossible. More than providing additions to foods or a connection to Italy, the garden gave time for Nonno to relax. After a long day of hard work, in the evening, he would water the pots on the fire escape and then weed a garden in a vacant lot.

In late fall, he added wine-making to his relaxing chores. Once a year, Nonno and several of the superintendents in the neighborhood pooled their limited resources and purchased grapes to make *vino rosso* (red wine). Only the tenement superintendents had the space in their basements to make wine, a benefit of their positions. Dominic "Watermelon's" green truck arrived with wooden crates of red grapes, the same truck in summer that contained watermelons sold by the slice. The baritone voice of its driver loudly announced the truck's arrival by the call of "*watermelone*," regardless of the time of year or the truck's contents.

The neighborhood wine-makers solemnly convened to select their grapes. All had to be present to begin the process, which took several hours. Visually inspecting, smelling, feeling, and tasting grapes from each crate, they compared them, which to the unskilled eye looked absolutely the same. Somehow, each vintner acquired exactly what he expected. My grandfather carried the chosen crates down to the crushing room, the dimly lit room adjacent to the building's tenant storage area. He opened the door, and feral cats inhabiting the area slunk away to hide, having never seen the sun or left the basement.

The basement became a winery. My grandfather took each crate, carefully sorting the grapes, eating or placing the rejects into a dented, scratched, black metal pot, which he later carried upstairs for family tasting. The remaining grapes he placed into a wooden circular container, the size of the bottom of a small barrel. Nonno cranked a rusted metal handle connected to a series of rusted gears that rose then lowered a rod connected to a mechanical disk, crushing the grapes. Siphoning off the fluid, he removed the remains and tasted the liquid.

Next, he carefully measured a white granular component, *un tipo di zucchero speciale* (special sugar), and added it to the liquid. The pressing continued, and he tasted the liquid again, adding more sugar until the liquid achieved the perfect mix. Then he poured the contents into a thirty-five-gallon wood cask, the same one used the year before and the year before that. Finally, he placed the cask on its side onto a wood rack with a cork inserted in its top and wax applied to the cork, indicating the wine-making process was now complete. Nonno stood, hands clasped, blue-gray eyes raised to the asbestos-pipe-covered heaven, saying a prayer never heard in church. Smiling, he turned off the basement lights, returning the area to its denizen inhabitants.

Nonno sampled the wine monthly or more frequently, waiting and waiting for the magic to occur and the special day to arrive. "*Un giorno il mio vino sarà il brindisi di Sullivan Street, un vino speciale, solo perle nozze e i battesimi.* (The day will come when my wine will be the toast of Sullivan Street, a special wine, drunk only for baptisms and weddings.)" Year after year, he repeated the process with always the same results—a harsh wine best mixed with cream soda or ginger ale or used on salads. No matter the outcome, never was a drop wasted. In fall when the wind increased and the temperature dropped, Nonno's thoughts turned to next year. "*Quest' anno, che è stato così freddo, avremo un' molto calda chedarebbe l'esatta quantità di zucchero all' uva, il vino sarà ottimo.* (This year, with this cold weather, we will have a hot summer, the grapes will have the right amount of sugar, and the wine will be the best.)" My grandfather looked to the future with hope and anticipation as he had fifty years ago, saving money for his family to come to America.

The owner of the tenement purchased an adjacent vacant lot on the corner of Sullivan and Prince Streets, containing the remains of a two-story building torn down due to disrepair. A rusted chain-link fence with locked gate surrounded the property. My grandfather had the key to the lock, one of many he wore on a large brass ring attached to his worn leather belt. In the rear of this vacant lot strewn with debris, he cleared a small patch of earth, freeing it from the concrete, rocks, rusted metal, and garbage. He turned over this patch of earth, adding coffee grounds from the café on the corner, vegetable waste from his table and neighborhood vegetable stores and pushcarts, shredded newspaper, and horse manure unknowingly donated by some of New York's finest mounted patrols.

This tall slender man with blue eyes, short white hair, dressed in threadbare brown pants with brown suspenders over a light blue chambray work shirt and red handkerchief around his neck, hands callused from the past seventy years, wrinkled brow beaded with sweat, stood in the lot, smiling at his sprouting treasures. He was a stern parent, expressing little if any emotion, yet in his garden, he beamed with yellowed teeth showing through his smiling lips. At five; my job was to help Nonno water the garden as he pointed to each plant, telling me its Italian name, asking me to repeat it while watering the plant.

Taking a rake, he smoothed the soil between the rows, then laid the rake on the ground to pull a weed while I attended to the watering. In my eagerness to make sure all the plants received enough water, I concentrated on dragging the hose around the corner of the row and forgot to watch where I was walking. Wham! I stepped on the rake, and it struck the ridge of my nose, causing blood to pour from both nostrils, and I began to cry. My grandfather, surprised, turned to see my bloody nose and tears. He reached down, picked me up, and taking the wet handkerchief from his neck, placed it on my nose. I stopped crying, and gradually both of us regained our composure. His blue eyes filled with concern as he hugged me. The bleeding stopped, signaling it was time to leave the magic garden. Nonno took the key from his brass ring and locked the gate, placing my small hand in his, and we began walking to 120 Sullivan Street, joined in thoughts of our recent adventure.

We climbed the two flights of stairs to Apartment #32. Before entering, Nonno squatted, now looking directly into my wet eyes, pointing to my sore nose. My grandfather moved his finger to his lips, saying in his best English, "Shush, shush!"

Entering the apartment and walking through the long, narrow, dark hallway, Nonno announced our arrival. My grandmother rose from her chair, entering the kitchen while Mom and Aunt Mamie conducted

Nonna and Nonno

their version of the Inquisition. "What did you do in the garden? Did you work hard for Nonno?" Nonno did not say a word. Heading to the icebox and taking out a bottle of cream soda, he presented a small glass to me. "*Grazie, grazie,*" he thanked me for working so hard in the garden, to the delight of my mother, grandmother, and aunt.

Our secret remained intact until today. Over the years, red wine found its way into my cream soda, and those hard blue eyes always had a little smile and a twinkle for me.

🏢🏬🏛🏚

Nonna, my grandmother Domenica, was two years younger and eight inches shorter than her husband. She wore her long white hair braided behind her head, on top of which she wore a black kerchief. Nonna's brown eyes stood out against the smooth milky white of her face, her smile a beacon of contentment, the family's lighthouse. Although my *nonno* spoke only on rare occasions, of the two, he was the chatterbox; Nonna's looks spoke paragraphs. Every morning with her children, she cleaned the tenement, sweeping, washing the hallways, stairs, entryway, and sidewalk. In the basement, she cleaned garbage cans, and stoked the coal furnace with a shovel taller then she. With the tenement chores complete, shopping and meal preparation began. She purchased vegetables from the pushcarts on Bleecker Street, walking to Thompson Street, selecting a live chicken, rabbit or pigeons from the market. Returning home with her butchered bounty, she began the family meal. If the menu included a chicken or pigeon, she removed the bird feathers prior to cooking, a time-consuming task that also required recleaning most of the kitchen afterwards.

Nonna's kitchen provided the stage for her nightly performances. The walls were rough plaster over lath, painted with yellow oil-based paint. A single light covered by a frosted glass bowl hung in the center of the ceiling, a pull cord attached to the fixture brought subdued light onto the stage. The rectangular wooden table with an enameled metal top and four white wooden chairs occupied the left wall together with an icebox, replaced later with a refrigerator. The wall to the right contained a porcelain sink with two basins, one covered by a corrugated porcelain removable top for drying dishes and pots and pans. The basin below the removable top also served as the apartment's baby bathtub and clothes washer. The clothes dryer was a clothesline stretched across the airshaft, operated by metal pulleys attached to the living room window frame.

A four-burner, white, gas range with a permanent, cast-iron kettle occupied the space next to the sink. Standing adjacent to the stove, only slightly taller, in black dress with buttons down the center, a white apron, and black kerchief was my *nonna*. Framing Nonna was the window to the fire escape and its packed garden.

My grandmother kept the meals simple, a necessity since the family had little money. The cuts of meat and available vegetables required seasoning and long cooking times to tenderize and flavor. As a cook, my nonna was a magician.

After school or playing in the street, I always stopped at Apartment #32 on my way up to Apartment #64. Entering the kitchen, Nonna stopped, cleaned her hands on her white apron always giving me a hug and salty wet kiss. Silently, Nonna stepped to the stove, carefully and dramatically lifting the lid on the big black kettle. She was so diminutive I wondered how she could lift the kettle on and off the stove.

Over the years, I discovered the shape of the utensil next to the kettle indicated what it contained. A light colored, small wooden spoon meant a tomato sauce was slowly simmering in the kettle. The tomato sauce contained both porcini mushrooms and pieces of chicken, but on Friday, a meatless day for Catholics, the sauce had only mushrooms, onions, and basil. A metal scoop with a flat handle and the kettle contents changed to minestrone soup, pasta *fagioli*, escarole soup with fagioli, or on days other than Friday, tiny meatballs in chicken soup.

"You never use a metal spoon with tomato sauce!" commanded Helen, the Head Aunt. "The tomatoes are acid and will eat away at the metal in the spoon, making the sauce taste like rusty nails." I never questioned the Head Aunt's cooking commandment until noticing the tomatoes in winter did not come from the fire escape garden or the plot in the vacant lot but from metal cans. I, as well as the entire family, knew better than to challenge Helen's cooking commandments or any of her other commandments.

If a dark brown, wooden dowel was in the kettle, my eyes grew wide in anticipation for this was Nonna's signature dish, polenta with mushroom sauce—creamy polenta spooned onto a plate and then covered with a thick sauce as much red as brown, sprinkled with pale yellow Locatelli cheese.

Regardless of the kettle's contents, Nonna always followed the same sampling ritual. First, she dipped her finger quickly into the kettle then put it to her mouth. Smiling, she took the wooden spoon coated with the kettle's contents and spread the sauce on a thin slice of day-old Italian bread on a cracked salad plate, the plate *soltanto per i parenti*, (used only for family). Nonna entered the walk-in pantry, taking out the wooden cheese-grating box. The box had a wooden drawer under a recessed metal cheese grater. She placed the box on the table, took out the drawer, putting the bread with brown red sauce on the cracked salad plate into the cheese box. From the refrigerator, she placed a wedge of Locatelli on the grate. Pale yellow white snow fell on the rose garden.

If I arrived when the kettle was not on the stove or its contents not ready for consumption, the cheese box remained in the pantry, but the Locatelli came out of the refrigerator. Off came a slice of cheese placed on day-old bread on a cracked salad plate for me to sample. Nonna's Sunday and holiday meals included homemade spinach, mushroom and cheese ravioli, each cut by hand from the flattened rolls of dough, a perfect one-inch square. My grandmother's vision began to deteriorate as she aged, but as she could neither read nor write, she had no need to visit the eye doctor. Meanwhile, the size of the ravioli increased; now only two or three ravioli sufficed for a meal.

Not all days contain only happiness; sadness touches everyone's life. Aunt Mamie, the youngest of their seven children, lived with Nonna and Nonno. In her mid thirties, engaged to be married, that same year, Mamie received a diagnosis of an aggressive facial cancer. Over the next four years, she underwent several surgeries to remove the cancer. She suffered excruciating pain, and eventually God delivered her from her suffering. Several weeks after the funeral, I came home from Saint Anthony's School. I stopped at Nonna's, running down the hallway as usual and into the kitchen. The stage was vacant. I found my nonna sitting on a straight-back wooden chair in the living room, looking out the window at the brick wall of the airshaft, ten feet away. No smile played across her lips, water welling in her eyes replaced the normal light. I leaned over her shoulder, tears in my eyes, and gave her a hug and wet salty kiss.

Both my grandparents never left the ten-block area of the neighborhood unescorted. When they needed to leave that familiar territory, a family member appointed by the Head Aunt accompanied them. Uncle Louie and Aunt Nettie had Nonna spend a week with them at the President Hotel in Long Island, a summer vacation getaway where they worked and lived. Nettie received a phone call while my grandmother was visiting. A client requested Nettie meet him and his wife in the hotel's lobby, a meeting estimated to consume half an hour. Nettie asking Nonna, "Mom, do you want to go to the lobby with me or stay here in the apartment?" Nonna, sitting on a chair facing the window to the main road, shook her head *no!* deciding to remain behind.

Aunt Nettie returned from the lobby twenty minutes later, finding her mother-in-law sobbing uncontrollably. Nettie wrapping arms around Nonna asking, "Were you thinking about Dad?" My grandmother shook her head no. Nettie asked, "Why are you crying?"

My grandmother looked up through the tears and, for her almost yelling, said, "*Sto diventando cieca, sto diventando cieca* (I am going blind; I am going blind)." Looking out the window, Nonna saw a light. "*Ho visto una luce rossa, e poi verde, sempre cambiando* (the light was red, then it was green, and it kept changing)."

Still holding her mother-in-law in her arms, Nettie began laughing, recognizing the indication of Nonna's "blindness"—a traffic light.

Nonno died in 1954 when Nonna was seventy-four years old. The family lovingly looked after her with daily visits. She spent time visiting with her sons and daughters.

Nonna died in 1960 at eighty. I still have her wood polenta dowel. Taking this wand in my hand, I see Nonna in her kitchen sixty years ago, smelling the Locatelli, tasting the mushroom sauce, naturally, on a slice of day-old Italian bread, served only on a cracked salad plate.

The DeVincenci's: Aunts Antoinetta, Mamie, and Helen;
Uncles Joe, Louie and Albert; Mom, Dad, and me

My Father's Parents

Dad's family came from the hills surrounding Naples. My grandfather, Giovanni Vivolo, left Apica, Beneventu, in 1886 at eighteen with little to his name. My grandmother, Mary Lapreta, born in America of immigrants, spoke some English, and grew up on Thompson Street with her immediate family and various relatives. Giovanni traveled to New York to meet his intended in an arranged marriage between the two families, something I never knew until a night with Dad at Porto Bello. My grandfather worked several years on various odd jobs, eventually becoming a barber. He married Mary, moving to an apartment on Grand Street. They had two children there, Aunt Rosie and my dad, Antonio. Then they moved to 57 Thompson Street to a larger apartment in the same building my grandmother had lived in growing up. There they had a third child, Anna, who died in an apartment fire. A coin-fed gas meter located in the hallway outside the apartment supplied fuel for the lights and stove. Anna, at two, was standing too close to a gas burner, and her clothes caught fire. The story over the years was always told with great sadness, fault never directed, though the heartbreak of losing a child was always with us.

Dad grew up on Grand and Thompson Streets. In his thirties, he married Elvira Ann DeVincenzi, moving to 120 Sullivan Street, into an apartment above his sister Rosie and her family. My grandmother Mary and my grandfather Giovanni, after my parents' honeymoon, moved in with my parents to the two-bedroom four-room apartment and stayed for the next twenty-two years. I was six when my grandmother Mary died. My memory of her is limited. At every holiday and on days that weren't, someone always told a story about my grandmother, causing laughter and heads shaking in disbelief for my grandmother had always approached life's challenges in ways unique and very different from her peers. Through these recollections, I felt she was with me growing up, as if I really knew this strong woman with a unique sense of humor.

My grandmother maintained a huge presence in our apartment. Tall and over two hundred pounds, she had the nickname Big Mamma. Her voice, laugh, and animated body language went with the name. Based on family stories, she evidently held the alpha female position of her time. Big Mamma helped care for both my cousins and me growing up. My cousins, who were older, had a longer relationship with her, and their memories reinforce the nickname. She cooked with Mom for our family, baking for both, having a gift for making the special breads and cookies for saint's feast days, Easter, and Christmas, treats only the rich could afford to purchase in the pastry shops. Big Mamma never just cooked a meal; she created culinary masterpieces. Holiday meals lived on beyond her death. Family members discussed her dishes in detail, setting a standard for excellence that continued into the future. After a particularly good meal, someone would always say, "It was good, but not as good as Big Mamma's."

In addition to caring for the family, she helped bring in income by doing piecework in the kitchen with Mom. Big Mamma and Mom sat at the kitchen table, covered with newspaper and pots of glue, making artificial flowers. The props on the table changed to needle and thread when sewing women's undergarments. Big Mamma possessed another talent for generating income—gambling. Our neighborhood was a miniature illegal Las Vegas. Big Mamma placed daily bets with bookies on numbers and horses, but her real passion was playing poker. My grandmother taught me to play five-card stud at five, beginning my graduate studies in gin before she died.

I heard stories of her staying up all night playing cards, on one occasion causing a disturbance, which became a legend in the neighborhood. My grandparent's apartment on Thompson Street was close to the roof, and the tenements abutted each other. When Big Mamma found it necessary to visit for a poker game in the adjacent tenement, she saved her energy for the game. Rather than descend four flights of stairs, then climb up three or four flights to the destination apartment, she used the roof. In her flowing black dress, large white apron, and black kerchief, she pushed and pulled herself over the building's three-foot brick walls surrounding the roof, walking down the stairs to the destination apartment. Once the game was over, she reversed the method of travel, returning to her apartment.

On one occasion, my grandmother played cards until five thirty in the morning then began her journey home. She was almost over the two brick walls when her black dress caught between them. She began pulling to free the dress but to no avail. Finally leveraging all her strength, she pulled herself free, ripping her dress in the process. As the dress ripped, she loudly voiced her displeasure by howling and swearing in Italian.

The animated swearing traveled through the open roof-top door to the milkman, who looked up to see a large black-and-white figure, hovering above the roof through the morning darkness. The milkman dropped the metal rack of glass milk bottles, screaming, "Ghost, ghost, ghost!" running down the four flights of stairs, and waking every tenant. Big Mamma became a legend on Thompson Street.

June thirteenth is the feast day of Saint Anthony of Padua, commemorated in the neighborhood by a ten-day street festival. Banners of saints decorated fire escapes. Flags of Italy, America, and Italian cities and towns lined both sides of Sullivan Street from Spring Street to Houston Street. Metal grids shaped as arches covered with multicolored lights spanned Sullivan Street from curb to curb, creating a luminescent tunnel in the darkness of the city. The sounds of Italian music and pop music created a backdrop for the crowds, gathering nightly in this two-block area. Sullivan Street remained closed both day and night, providing access for only emergency vehicles and supply and maintenance trucks.

Booths constructed with two by fours, covered with colorful heavyweight canvas or plastic tarps, lined the street. Catering to the neighborhood's needs, they sold sausage sandwiches with onions and peppers finely chopped and cooked on a propane gas grill, the sausages on a charcoal fire. Smoke and the cooking aroma combined together, attracting the hungry. The peppers, onions, and sausage were combined and placed into sliced Italian bread that struggled to contain its new arrivals. The sandwich was wrapped in white butcher paper and handed to the recipient. A neighborhood vendor at an adjacent booth took dough the size of golf balls, placing each into a kettle of hot oil over a propane gas burner, the hot oil turning the dough golden brown. He removed the brown soft balls from the kettle and set them into a perforated metal pan to drain. For a mere quarter, five hot *zeppole* covered with white powered sugar and placed into a brown paper bag were yours. Pizza by the slice, calzones, watermelon slices, spumoni, lemon ice, popcorn, cotton candy, soda, and beer filled out the menu.

Adjacent booths provided games of chance for the daring or skilled: three darts for a quarter to throw at a board filled with balloons. Break three balloons and the stuffed giant panda bear was yours. Three softballs to throw at milk bottles, three wooden rings to toss over empty coke bottles in wooden racks, and my favorite, three ping-pong balls to toss for a quarter at circular bowls filled with colored water and goldfish. Landing a ping-pong ball by skill, by chance, or by prayer into a bowl put the bowl, colored water, and goldfish into your hands—and once, into mine.

Proudly I took the results of my efforts up to Apartment #64. Displaying my prowess, I was met with oohs and ahhs from Mom. Dad asked, "How many ping-pong balls did you toss?"

"About nine or twelve, I think."

"That's about a buck for the goldfish bowl that costs about a nickel, the goldfish that costs a penny or two, and the water that's free."

Regardless of whether it took one or twenty ping-pong balls, the goldfish never made it beyond twenty-four hours. We needed no autopsy to determine death caused by overfeeding, not surprising in an Italian family.

The feast of Saint Anthony wasn't about food, games of chance, or music; the feast was about Saint Anthony and the church. A procession on the first day of the feast, started behind the church, headed south down Thompson Street to Broome Street, west on Broome to Sullivan, up Sullivan back to the church. The color guard and band led the procession. Band members, dressed in brown pants, white, wide-collared shirts, and red scarves, played trumpets, mandolins, trombones, accordions, flutes, and a tuba. The most important part of the band was the big bass drum, the last one in line and the only one in that line.

A priest in a brown cassock with leather sandals carried a six-foot-high brass crucifix, flanked by two altar boys with three-foot brass candleholders and candles, which continually lost their flame, causing the procession to halt until the candles were relit. Next, came the altar boys dressed in their black robes and white surplices for high mass, looking as solemn as ten- and twelve-year-olds in our neighborhood could, followed by the Franciscan sisters of Saint Anthony's School having much to do with the solemnity of the altar boys. The nuns joined with the choir of grade school boys and girls in robes, singing Latin responses to the priests' and brothers' litanies following the choir. A life-size statue of Saint Anthony marked the finale, his simple clothing of a brown Franciscan robe contrasting with that of his bearers, eight members of the Knights of Columbus, decked out in ceremonial dress of gold hats with white plumes, a gold sash over a white shirt, navy blue pants, and ceremonial swords.

As the procession wound its way through the neighborhood, the collector of offerings from each tenement presented an envelope to the head of the Knights of Columbus, wearing a navy blue ceremonial cape. Each envelope had written upon it in fine calligraphy or printing the tenement's address, the amount donated, and the person designated as collector. After duly recording the information into an official gold book he carried together with his sword, the leader of the Knights pinned the envelope to the brown cassock of Saint Anthony.

The amounts collected in each tenement became an unintentional neighborhood competition. Every year the amount collected from 120 Sullivan Street was significantly less than the other tenements, a fact intentionally and unintentionally made known to everyone in the neighborhood. After putting up with negative comments for several years about the Genovese holding tight to each buck—"Hey I can see Washington crying; he must have hated to leave your wallet" or "Look at Lincoln; his eyes are closed; he died trying to leave the Genovese wallet"—Big Mamma had enough, volunteering to become the offering collector for 120 Sullivan Street for next year's feast.

After contacting everyone in the building for donations, the amount collected was only slightly higher than the preceding years. Big Mamma initiated a creative method for obtaining donations; she founded the "Novena of Poker Games for Saint Anthony," nine games scheduled and played in 120 Sullivan Street prior to the beginning of the feast. Ten percent of every pot was placed into the collection envelope. On the day of the procession, Big Mamma presented the envelope from 120 Sullivan, containing donations and poker pot contributions, to the leader of the Knights of Columbus. He duly recorded the results and pinned the envelope to Saint Anthony's cassock. The collected donation from 120 Sullivan did not place in the top ten, but the results provided respectful silence for its residents and a unique method for collecting offerings.

Big Mamma, together with two women in the tenement, was often summoned to assist and bring peace to the sick. My grandmother believed sickness was attributed to Malocchio (the Evil Eye), caused by someone who was jealous, wishing you evil. She believed it necessary to remove the evil wished upon you in order for you to get well. Once when I was sick with fever for several days, my mother summoned the family doctor. After his examination and his consumption of coffee and Italian pastries, he gave me an injection of penicillin, causing me to cry. The next day, I continued to run a low fever. Apparently the time schedule my grandmother had for my recovery had passed, and the doctor's medicine, she decided, needed help.

That night, Big Mamma together with Rosie "Nap," her *paesana* from the third floor, carrying rosaries, began lighting candles around my bed on the living room couch. Mom turned out the lights, Rosie and my grandmother knelt down beside me, chanting in Italian. While praying, they placed their forefingers into a bowl of olive oil and garlic and then anointed my forehead with the sign of the cross. They placed bay leaves on my forehead and throat after rubbing them into the oil and garlic. At first, I was mystified by the ceremony, *a fare gli occhi* (to make the eyes). But as the ceremony continued, I became frightened and cried. The prayers abruptly ended, the lights came on, candles blown out, and Rosie "Nap" left. I stopped crying, and things settled down. Big Mamma came back to the living room with a bowl of chocolate ice cream and Italian butterfly cookies. She placed them before me saying, "Don't be scared; you will get better now," and I did.

Papa John and Big Mamma occupied the back bedroom. After she died, my grandfather continued living with my parents for another twenty years. As his wife was nicknamed Big Mamma, a contrasting "Little John" suited him. He was short and slight of stature, weighing all of 120 pounds. During his life in our apartment, I never remember my grandfather working his trade as a barber or even leaving the building. Even his visits to his daughter's apartment, one story below, were limited. After Papa John had a stroke, impairing his right arm and hand, he required a cane to walk and assistance when small muscle activity was required. He had other limitations, one being a hernia, compared to my son's but, "è *il doppio di quella di mio figlio e piu fastidiosa* (twice the size and more of a problem)." He wore an elastic and metal truss to hold the hernia in place. The hernia became an excellent excuse for avoiding the activities he did not want to do, which were many.

Papa John, on most days, wore slippers, dark blue pants, a white long john top, white dress shirt, and a dark blue striped vest. The vest pockets held a gold pocket watch with gold chain, a corncob pipe, tobacco, and matches. He lit the pipe after breakfast, lunch, and dinner, times varying slightly over the years due to holidays and special visitors. Papa John's breakfast consisted of a cup of black coffee, topped off with a shot of grappa; a piece of yesterday's Italian bread; and a fried egg over which he crumbled a piece of dried hot red pepper. A string of dried peppers hung from the metal grate outside his bedroom window.

After dinner, he poured himself another glass of wine and lit one of his Italian stogies. The stogies were six-inch, rolled, coarse tobacco cigars, which he fermented in a jar containing grappa and anisette and then removed and dried a minimum of two weeks before use. After watching this stogie ritual night after night as a teenager, I decided to try smoking one on the twilight rooftop of 120 Sullivan Street. I put the stogie in the center of my mouth, using my teeth as clamps, and lit up. After two or three puffs, I could feel my lungs surging then quickly recoiling, my head growing hollow, and the sound of my breathing now a loud booming echo. I became convinced stogies were better suited to keeping away mosquitoes and cockroaches than for smoking

Papa John spoke slowly and only in Italian, using hand and eye signals to convey intent. Conversations turned into games of charades with no subject guessed in less than five minutes. I never heard him speak or attempt to speak English. The closest he came to speaking English was in calling my name, and even that had an Italian accent. I assumed he had immigrated many years after the rest of the family, but later I discovered he had preceded every family member by over ten years. Papa John stubbornly decided he would speak only one language; if Italian was good enough for his father, it was good enough for him. Frequently loud discussions ensued between Papa John and Big Mamma about anything, such as which shape of pasta was appropriate for the evening's sauce. The arguments began on the slightest disagreement, and the longer they lasted the louder and wilder they became. He presented his side, of course, in Italian, she in a loud forceful mixture of English and Italian. Eventually, arms and hands were whirling, heads swaying in many directions, and we, their audience, laughing, which subsequently dropped the curtain on the discussion. When Papa John for the first time, heard the Italian lyrics of "Nel Blu De Pinto De Blu (Volare)" on the radio, he looked up smiling with tears running from his blue-green eyes, his values confirmed; everyone will speak only Italian just like him.

🏢

Living in a city packed with people, in apartments with no room to spare, we made use of every available space we could. Fire escapes became our gardens; rooftops became an escape of sorts. They provided a place to tan during a hot summer day, a place to sleep in the only breeze at night. The roof provided sanctuary, an escape from people and noise, a place to be alone. In a city of tenements, this was our backyard. The roof was a vantage point to see the entire sky not just a skinny piece of it, a place where you could witness sunrise and sunset, extending for miles not just a few feet as seen from the window, if you were lucky enough to have one. Looking down from the roof onto the images in the street below was looking into the clear plastic window of an ant farm. The rooftop was the only room with a view, without ceiling, without walls, without noise, without people, without limits for mind or soul.

They also held secrets revealed only to a few.

A few years after Big Mamma died, an unplanned Christmas gift from my uncles, a puppy, joined our family. Both my parents had fears about being evicted for harboring an unregistered dog in our apartment. My grandfather protested the longest and loudest, using his cane to tell the puppy about its heritage. The pup got to stay and slept under the kitchen sink, relegated to the kitchen, which also happened to be Papa John's domain. When the pup came out from the sink close to my grandfather's chair, the cane quickly and forcefully declared the territorial boundary.

The pup, trained not to bark, keeping his presence a secret, used the roof as a bathroom and exercise yard, thereby avoiding discovery and eviction. The dog lived for ten years, only leaving the apartment once, going to Sullivan Street in a cardboard box to get shots from a vet. The vet's visit was on a Saturday at 8 a.m., early enough not to attract attention. As Skippy got older, it took him longer to decide on each visit to the roof which square foot of over five thousand square feet of roof he would feel affection for and visit. During the winter, once

Skippy on the roof
with me

Big Mamma, Mom, me, Papa John, and Dad

absentmindedly left on the roof and finally retrieved, he entered the apartment, greeting Papa John with an ice-cold nose. I then learned a new Italian swear word from my grandfather. Twice a week, I cleaned the roof with a brown paper bag to prevent leaving clues that could result in eviction.

One afternoon, released early by the nuns from grade school, I tore up the stairs to change clothes to play in the street with my friends. As I entered the hallway, I heard mumblings in the kitchen and quietly approached. Papa John had his good hand on the dog's head as it sat next to him, quietly talking to the dog as he sometimes did to me. Papa John looked up and smiled; we may have had the only bilingual dog in New York City. When Papa John passed away, the dog still resided in the kitchen, sitting and lying by Papa John's chair, searching for the thin hand that stroked him most of the day.

Rooftops held more creatures than dogs. Uncle Louie raised and flew pigeons and maintained pigeon coops on roofs from his youth to his late fifties. They fascinated me, and I decided to try my hand at this newfound sport. I built a small pigeon coop in the basement of our building, constructing it in two parts in order to carry it up the six sets of stairs to the roof. To avoid eviction, I hid the coop behind steel girders that had previously supported the wood stave water tank that originally provided water for fighting fires in the building. I placed two pigeons, tumblers—one white and gray, the other brown—in the coop. I stored the pigeon food under Papa John's bed. My grandfather watched each step of this project, objecting by vigorously shaking his head, closing his eyes and raising them to heaven, pointing to the ceiling with his cane saying in his loudest Italian, "*Questo non è una buon'idea.* (This is not a good idea.)"

One afternoon my mother announced she was going to use her carpet sweeper and clean the apartment floor. Silent fear gripped and held Papa John and me captives. She pushed the wheeled sweeper down the dark hallway through each room, nearing the back bedroom, Papa John's room. Panic suddenly set in; my grandfather and I envisioned a carpet sweeper ripping open a thirty-five pound bag of pigeon food. I ran to the back bedroom, causing skid marks on the linoleum. My grandfather stood at the foot of his bed, waving his cane high above Mom's head, telling my mother "*No! No! Non adesso!* (No! No! Not now!)" My mother, startled by my grandfather's agitation and loud voice, stopped, turning back down the hallway, shaking her head. Mom returned the carpet sweeper back to the closet rather than potentially causing another stroke. Papa John looked at me with a smile, knowing he had committed a mortal sin, and winked in affirmation.

I continued this hobby, several years later housing pigeons on a warehouse roof on 521 Broome Street. Access to the warehouse required climbing to the top of the tenement at 529 Broome Street and then using a ten-foot wooden ladder to access the top of the adjacent warehouse roof. Once on that roof, all you had to do was scramble over two four-foot-high walls to 521 and the pigeon coop. I was working a summer job with Walsh Trucking, delivering metal pipe and cast-iron fittings. At the end of our Friday trip, I bought four pigeons in Green Point, Brooklyn. Placing the pigeons in a cardboard box, we headed for the garage on Sullivan Street. Approaching Sullivan Street, the weather changed, the wind increased, darkness set in, and rain began cascading onto the concrete and asphalt, backing up the gutters. With daylight quickly vanishing, I decided not to put the pigeons into the coop and, instead, took the cardboard box up five flights of stairs to our apartment.

I left the box in the hallway, electing to face eviction rather than face my parents. Entering the apartment, I silently washed for dinner. After dinner we cleaned the dishes, took out the garbage, and Papa John went to bed. Mom took the dog up to the roof for his nightly visitation. Upon returning with the wet dog, Mom questioned me about the box in the hallway.

I explained the situation. "It's just for tonight. I'll get up early and take the pigeons up to the coop."

Mom, concerned with a possible eviction, said, "Take the pigeons from the hallway and put them in the bathtub." She and dad did not like that solution but preferred it to the alternative and accepted since it was only for one night. After much discussion, Mom, Dad, and I went to bed, having no better solution to our current problem, leaving the pigeons in the bathtub in the dark bathroom.

At two in the morning, I awoke to a loud string of Italian swear words. Circling the kitchen, attempting a landing on top of the kitchen cabinets, were three of the four pigeons; the fourth confronted in full flight the shade over the kitchen window. At the sink below the cabinets was Dad in white boxer shorts, hernia belt, and sleeveless undershirt swinging a broom in the direction of the nearest pigeon approaching the cabinet. Papa John, in long johns and hernia belt, pointed with his cane, shaking it vehemently at the pigeons in flight while all the time expressing himself in Italian expletives. Mom was at the kitchen table ripping pieces of Wonder bread, throwing them on the floor saying, "Here pigeon, pigeon." Papa John had arisen in the middle of the night and turned on the lights in the bathroom. Seeing the cardboard box and hearing a rattle within, he had cautiously opened it with his cane and let forth the nighttime entertainment.

The next night after dinner, Mom and Dad left to visit Aunt Rosie. Papa John then looked at me across the table over his second glass of wine, lighted a stogie, shook his head, smiling, and said, "*Basta congli uccelli, Basta!* (No more birds, no more!)"

Author flying pigeons on Broome Street

The Rooftop

Far from the canyons of the city
Above the clamor

An isolated humanity
Immaculate of classification

Expanse of sky
And sunlight

Uninterrupted flight
Of bird and man

Chill wind, clean snow
Mind and matter unite

Solitude and space
Free the soliloquies

Sanctuary from
The frenzy below

Aunt Rosie

Not only did I have two sets of grandparents living with us, I was lucky to have three fathers, three mothers, and an "extra" sister. Living in the apartment directly beneath us was Dad's older sister, her husband, and their three children. Rosie and Jimmy Rosso became surrogate parents.

Aunt Rosie and Uncle Jimmy lived on the fourth floor of 120 Sullivan Street in Apartment #54 for over forty-five years. They raised their children Jamsie, Rosemary, and Anthony in the two-bedroom apartment directly below us, the layout of which matched ours exactly and served as an extension of our own and others in the neighborhood. Opening the dark brown outer door, you entered a four-foot-wide hallway with a ten-foot ceiling lit by a single forty-watt light bulb. To the left of the entrance door was the bathroom with bathtub, sink, and toilet; four feet further down the hall also to the left was the back bedroom with a window opening to one of the building's airshafts. The room contained a three-foot walk-in closet, the only one in the apartment. Eight feet further, the hallway turned ninety degrees to the left. Directly beyond the turn to the right, a door opened to the second bedroom with a window opening to Sullivan Street. Six more feet down the hallway and to the left was the kitchen with a window to the same airshaft as the back bedroom. Turning right from the kitchen was the living room with two windows onto Sullivan Street. The apartment was somewhat L shaped approximately twenty by twenty-five feet, a total of five hundred square feet.

Traffic up and down the flight of stairs between Apartments #54 and #64 became so significant during the holidays that we needed a traffic signal but made do with shouted directions. Aunt Rosie's apartment served as the gathering place for family, tenants from the building, and friends from the neighborhood. Money was scarce so people found entertainment by meeting in apartments, talking, laughing, and sharing food and drink, listening to the radio, and playing cards. Hearing voices and laughter, I ran through the open door down the hallway through the kitchen into the living room to see who was there. Relatives, neighbors, and friends sat around the big table, telling stories, some old, some new but always filling the room with joy and laughter, making everyday special.

Aunt Rosie was as small as Papa John but had the biggest perpetual smile and laugh, with a voice larger than the body in which it resided. Rosie always focused on the joys of life, raising the endorphin levels of all those within hearing distance. Rosie was the "scout"; with smiling dark eyes, she made first contact with new arrivals, putting them quickly at ease with her warmth and humor. Everyone remembered Rosie; once you spent time with her, she became a part of you, a free spirit, a memory cherished for a lifetime.

Big Mamma's personality definitely influenced Rosie's philosophy of life, but unlike her mother's that embraced just family, Rosie's extended beyond to the entire neighborhood. She became family to everyone she encountered, always easily adoptable. In Italian families, male members always received great respect, everyone deferring to them for their opinion or final word, the word becoming dogma. Not in our family. Rosie, with her charm and sense of humor, "Told it like it was," or as she thought it should be, always with such style that even the victim, in many cases my dad, laughed as hard as the rest of us. Aunt Rosie's sense of humor and outrageous comments did not stop with her brother; young and old, male and female experienced it. Laughter was a permanent sound in Apartment 54.

Aunt Rosie

Rosie, Big Mamma, Rosie Nap, Rosie Tomato Sauce, and Mom were daily customers of the storefront café in 120 Sullivan Street. It gave them a place to have an espresso, laugh, talk to friends, watch the kids playing in the street, store grocery bags, and rest a little before making the three to five flights of stairs to their apartments. Sometimes, actually most of the time, they pooled their resources, betting a horse by its name, playing daily numbers based on dates of birth, feast days, or death notice dates. Even license plate numbers gave suggestions for picking winners. Dreams, discussed and analyzed for hidden numbers and names, provided additional guidance for betting.

Aunt Rosie was the ringleader of the group, encouraging trips to Macy's or Gimbels, trips to the movies, dinners in Chinatown, and a beer at Shorty's bar on Prince Street. Rosie scheduled piecework meetings for the group every two weeks, making artificial flowers or sewing women's undergarments at the kitchen table. The women received payment the next day from the nearby factory for each completed piece. Once finished with the project, Rosie and crew cleared the kitchen table. Now feeling flush with potential cash, the women's poker games began with much laughter.

We spent all or most of the holidays downstairs with my aunt, uncle, and cousins. My aunt had a dining room table in her living room, seating twelve people; the kitchen sat four, only three comfortably. The big table was an extension of the kitchen, creating in a small two-bedroom apartment a miniature great room. Rosie and Jimmy's door was always open, the big table seating family and friends with kids exiled to the kitchen, adults having first dibs on big table seats.

Holidays and meals for special occasions were elaborate, filled with never-ending courses, primi and secondi increasing to *nove*; antipasti, soup, salad, macaroni or ravioli or lasagna, the "gravy" with sausage, meatballs, pork, beef, and *braciole*, or fish, clams, and mussels. *Then* came the main course—a capon, turkey, or roast beef, stuffed breast of veal, stuffed squid—and the vegetables and finally dessert and after-dinner drinks accompanied by fruit and cheese. Meals lasted several hours with snacks and leftovers offered after the meal, if you were still hungry.

The card game

Aunt Rosie, a good cook, always enjoyed socializing more than cooking. It became common to see whiffs of smoke escape from the door of the gas oven. One of us kids loudly reported the situation to Aunt Rosie, while the rest of the big-table exiles smiled, laughing in anticipation of the expected outcome. Rosie, in due course, finished her conversation, calmly walked to the kitchen, looked at the oven, and with hands on hips and dark brown eyes on the ceiling, smiled, and asked so all could hear, "Who turned up the temperature on the oven?" Then to the same ceiling, she loudly demanded, "Don't do it again!"

She removed the oven contents, beginning to serve from numerous platters and plates to everyone at the big table. "These will have to do; there is nothing else. If you want more, I'll make you a sandwich." The big table and the kitchen table simultaneously erupted with laughter, giggles, and praise. Young and old alike sought the culinary prize—the corner of the lasagna, the end of the roast, or the potatoes at the edge of the pan, whatever the cause of the smoke—all desired for their extra crispiness.

After Uncle Jimmy's death Rosie continued to cook with the same intensity, volume, and inattention. The building owner had smoke alarms installed in all the apartments to meet city building code requirements, probably due to my aunt's culinary skill. Dad, now also alone, still lived in the apartment above his sister. The telephone rang several times a week, Rosie exclaiming to her brother, "Come down and kill the damn bird!" It was my father's job in his late seventies to stand on a chair with a broomstick and hit the silence button on Rosie's screeching fire alarm.

Dad and I sometimes had dinner with Aunt Rosie at the big table in the living room, although we numbered only three. Despite the cold outside, the room filled with warmth from the remembered voices and laughter of former inhabitants of the big table. The guests, oblivious to time, heard their names spoken and stood before us as they had decades ago, causing smiles and memories each of us cherished.

After Uncle Jimmy died, Rosie allowed her youngest son Anthony to move back into her home. Uncle Jimmy had forcefully removed him from the apartment ten years earlier. My aunt during these ten years had kept track of her son through neighborhood contacts. I remember my cousin Anthony "Sidecar," a happy gentle giant, spending time teaching me to play baseball, making scooters using a two by four, an apple crate, and an old roller skate, always with a smile in his soft brown eyes. The eyes changed over the years to bloodshot; the smile became a grimace. My cousin was mainlining "H" (heroin), as were others in the neighborhood, some never making it out of alleys and basements due to overdoses. My uncle gave his son several opportunities, enrolling him in rehab programs, spending time with him, visiting him in various prisons, and always welcoming him back to Apartment #54. All to no avail for "Sidecar" took anything of value to support his habit. My uncle knew the odds of rehabilitation and the difficulty of overcoming addiction to heroin. The decision to ban him from the apartment was not easy but necessary once he accepted "Sidecar's" habit had become uncontrollable.

When my uncle died, "Sidecar" moved back in. Aunt Rosie at almost eighty became a mom again. She managed to have him enrolled in a rehab program as a prerequisite to his living with her. He enrolled in a methadone clinic on Eight Avenue. My aunt exhausted eighty years of neighborhood contacts to transport my cousin to the clinic once a week. Rosie, now frail with severe arthritis, did not leave her apartment, although much of the apartment contents left. During summer break, Rosie asked me several times to take my cousin to his clinic. I discovered "Sidecar" was not the cousin I had played with growing up. I'm not sure who he was, eyes and mouth closed, sitting or lying on the couch until I said, "It's time to leave; let's get going." The eyes with pinpoint pupils opened slowly together with the mouth; the tongue tested the air then checked the lips to insure that both were connected. The being found its voice, hostile, belligerent, then without warning, the eyes and mouth closed, and "Sidecar" had already left on another trip to somewhere.

During the visits, I saw my cousin for what he had become. My aunt saw him still as what he had been—in second grade at Saint Anthony's school—providing the same love, nurturing, and care that she had years before. Seeing him on the streets adjacent to the clinic where dealers clustered to sell drugs to the continuous stream of addicted visitors,

Rosemary, me, and Anthony (Sidecar)

getting their methadone and then making a hit, "Sidecar" was a familiar customer. Although I loved my aunt, a visit to the clinic once a week was more than I wanted to deal with, but I never said the words, only hoped she could read my mind.

Six months later, sitting with Dad at his kitchen table on the night I arrived, I asked about my cousin. Shaking his head, Dad said, "He hit the bottom, kid. You know he even pushed Aunt Rosie, and she had to call the cops. He left before they came. Nobody has seen him since. That was three months ago." No one in the family ever mentioned my cousin again; for them, "Sidecar" has disappeared.

Everyone in the neighborhood sang—Gregorian hymns at Saint Anthony's Church on Sundays at ten o'clock high mass, doo-wop in the tenement hallways. Every function with friends and family became an opportunity to sing. Aunt Rosie claimed she had been a singer in her twenties. Listening to her accompany the radio, I questioned her talent, although her delivery was superb. She sang everyday into her eighties with her radio voice coaches, Ella, Billy, and Ertha, even singing with the guys, Frank and Tony. Watching her sing, I witnessed magic in the making as she put her soul in every word, creating a world of joy even when singing the blues. Regardless of the song, her dark eyes danced as two beautiful costumed showgirls and delighted her audience with their every move.

Rosie worked at the funeral parlor, owned by Uncle Jimmy at 188 Bleecker Street on the corner of MacDougal and Bleecker, about two and a half blocks from their apartment, from ten until four during the week and as needed on the weekend. Death in our neighborhood was taken quite seriously. Custom dictated that the immediate family dress in black, display blank facial expressions, show no outward merriment, and refrain from playing the radio or television. Silence, prayer, mourning, and grieving were expected. On rare occasions it was OK, even encouraged, to proclaim grief and sorrow by yelling, screaming, waving arms wildly, while sobbing uncontrollably. The louder and wilder the outward expression, the more grief you had.

In the funeral parlor, the deceased lay in an open casket for three days of rosaries, prayers, and solemn visits by family, friends, and others in the neighborhood paying respect. A group of women from the neighborhood visited every funeral parlor, praying, weeping profusely and loudly, and then paying their respect to the family of the deceased, even though no one knew who they were. Rosie would announce from the office, "The women with the onions on their chest are here again."

Aunt Rosie was there to greet mourners, attend to the needs of the family of the deceased, and make all comfortable in their time of need. My aunt knew everyone in the neighborhood, and her warmth showed in greeting visitors as they arrived. Many times mourners elected to stay in the parlor office, talking solemnly or laughing with Rosie after signing the visitation book and never viewing the open casket.

Having a telephone in the early 1950s made Jimmy and Rosie the progressive members of the family and most of the neighborhood. The rest of us continued to use radiators and steam pipes to transmit cryptic messages to other apartment occupants. Striking risers and radiators with a knife sent "tenement telegraph," the correspondent's version of Morse code, to its recipient. The residents of 120 Sullivan Street used the telephone in Apartment #54 when it was necessary to send messages to those outside the building and outside the range of the building's piping system. One story above in Apartment #64, a phone, television, and toaster finally appeared a decade later.

Rosie and Jimmy even had Apartment #54 rewired with a large fuse box, sustaining not only a toaster but also an air conditioner and TV. Aunt Rosie's apartment, by neighborhood standards, was new and "with it." I was a permanent fixture downstairs on Friday and Saturday nights, entertained by television and enthralled by Apartment #54's world filled with magic and wonder.

My visits also exposed me to my aunt and uncle's different perspective on life, which often saw more than just wonderment in the world beyond the little one of Sullivan Street. My aunt and uncle, as a part of their business, met with many people from outside the neighborhood, which allowed them to feel comfortable in unfamiliar situations and to learn from these encounters about views different from their own.

On graduating from St. Anthony's Grade School at 60 MacDougal Street, I received a scholarship from a neighborhood organization to

Xavier High School, a Jesuit military prep school at Seventeenth Street in New York City. My friends were attending different high schools in the city and wanting to be with them, I decided not to accept the scholarship or show my parents the letter. After dinner on Friday night, I went down to Aunt Rosie's to watch TV. Only Rosie was in the apartment. Before putting on the TV, she asked about my day at school, "Where are you going to go to high school?" I told her about the letter, the partial scholarship, and how I had decided not to go there and not tell my parents.

Rosie listened, saying nothing, walking into her kitchen, loudly washing pots, pans, and dishes. She turned off the water, walked into the living room, and stood directly in front of me, blocking my view of the TV. With one hand on her apron and the other lying flat on the table, her dark eyes became pointed fingers as she asked me, "Do you know how many numbers you would have to hit to pay for that scholarship?"

I shook my head no.

Rosie took her hand off the table. Her back stiffened. Eyes still focused at me, she added, "You would have to hit the number for a hundred bucks twelve times in a row to make that much money. Never has that happened in this neighborhood." She walked back to the kitchen, ending our discussion.

I woke the next morning and ran down to Rosie's, asking her to telephone Xavier and see if it was not too late to accept the scholarship. It took some time to reach a person to discuss our problem after she explained why she had called. Silence. The noise of a stickball game in the street filled the apartment. Then Rosie, smiling, turned to me and said, "They still will accept you if you apply; it's not too late." That phone call was one of the most important calls of my life, thanks to my surrogate mom.

Many, many years later, Dad called to report that Aunt Rosie was in a hospital on Nineteenth Street and Third Avenue in New York City. I arrived the next day by "redeye" from Seattle. We spent most of the week at the hospital. The last day of my visit we went back to see Rosie. We spent the afternoon at the hospital, making small talk as best we could, hiding our true emotions. Dad stood and picked up his hat, signaling it was time to say our goodbyes. My father knowingly gave his big sister a hug and a kiss, turned quickly, and walked out of the room, wiping his eyes

In this hospital bed, in a gown that was much too big, sat a little brown-eyed girl, looking more like ten years old than eighty. I gently bent over her. "I love you very, very much. Thank you for being a mother to me. I love you." She looked up, holding back tears in her frightened eyes, and whispered, "I love you very much, too."

Uncle Jimmy

Uncle Jimmy looked like a neighborhood native, five foot seven, stout with hairy muscular arms, rough featured face, big head, large nose, and receding hairline. Self-educated, articulate, intelligent, streetwise with deep-set, dark, penetrating, brown eyes, he held his own in conversations, staring through you, challenging you. Those eyes sparkled when he listened, brightening all the more as the difference of opinion increased. Unlike most of the rest of us, Jimmy felt as comfortable in the world outside of Sullivan Street as within it.

Owning one of the four neighborhood funeral parlors made Uncle Jimmy successful. But his achievement never went to his head. He respected people, understood their needs, believed in them, and worked to meet their expectations. In the late 1920s, he had assisted immigrants and first-generation Italians to insure a proper burial. Many times, he purchased gravesites for families financially unable to, in turn receiving monthly payments without interest, which the family could afford. He arranged for the funeral mass and scheduled transportation for all family members to and from the mass and cemetery.

Besides being the first to get the latest technology, Uncle Jimmy and Aunt Rosie stood out in remodeling their apartment. No one in the neighborhood ever thought about bothering with such work. "Why? You're renting." "What you have is what you got and what you live with." At twelve, I thought Rosie and Jimmy's apartment represented the culmination of all the talents of the artisans of the mid 1900s. Only when I was married and in my thirties, having worked on my own house, did I recognize flaws in the remodel.

Uncle Jimmy believed in supporting the neighborhood by hiring only neighborhood people for his remodeling work whenever possible. He respected them, never questioning them. "They are from the neighborhood; that's why I hired them."

The hallway and several rooms were remodeled and covered with four-by-eight-foot wood paneling, scribed with vertical groves every six or eight inches to resemble actual wood boards. Since the ceiling measured approximately ten feet high, a second piece of paneling was needed below the first to reach the floor. A finishing strip covered the gap between the two, but the carpenter did not attempt to match the panels' vertical scribing. So, an eight-inch board above the finishing strip aligned with a six-inch or four-inch board below.

The bathroom, prior to construction, had a one-by-three-foot window opening to an airshaft. The window, to the right of the sink and left of the toilet, was set back about two feet and not easily accessible to open or close. Uncle Jimmy and Aunt Rosie had the bathroom paneled, and a sheet of paneling and the carpenter's magic hammer made the window disappear.

Because Uncle Jimmy and Aunt Rosie had the first television in the building in the early 1950s, on most Friday nights, I sat next to my cousin Rosemary watching shows until nine o'clock. Then Uncle Jimmy watched one of his favorite programs, Gillett's *Boxing, Cavalcade of Sports*. Jimmy, like every male in the neighborhood and some grandmothers from Naples, was an avid sports fan. My uncle quoted win-loss records and strengths and weaknesses of both fighters. Jimmy discussed the referee's performance as well. He focused on the referee's calls, which he perceived incorrectly influenced the outcome of the fight. His knowledge of baseball equaled that of boxing, though with less passion. As the apartment's sportscaster, Jimmy gave a dissertation after every round of every fight and every inning of every baseball game. A similar critical analysis preceded every poker and gin game, rolling his

Mom, Dad, Cousin Jamsie, and Uncle Jimmy in our kitchen

eyes to the heavens, smiling, shaking his head, questioning the logic or lack thereof of the player who drew to an inside straight taking his full house card. The players retort being laughter then responding, "You're an undertaker, go dig a good deep hole for yourself and jump in." "Take your full house card with you." "Give us a break."

One Friday night, at the magic hour of nine, Uncle Jimmy was not in the apartment. Aunt Rosie explained that Jimmy and his pal Phil were at Madison Square Garden, having tickets to the Jersey Joe Walcott, World Heavyweight Championship Fight. We turned on the TV, knowing we would see Uncle Jimmy. The fight began. But much to everyone's amazement, Walcott was knocked out in less than two minutes of the first round. We waited for Uncle Jimmy to return, anxious to hear his analysis of the fight. At eleven thirty, the door opened. My uncle walked into the room, poured himself a glass of wine, and without saying a word, sat down opposite us.

We pummeled him with questions. "Was it an uppercut?"

"Did Walcott see the punch?"

"Where was the referee?"

Uncle Jimmy raised his voice, "Stop!" Standing up with face red, his eyes glared in the direction of any noise or movement. Then he sat back down, serious and quiet as he glared at the ceiling. Finally, Jimmy said, "We had problems parking. We were walking down to our fifty-dollar seats when everyone in the Garden stood up, screaming. We didn't see the fighters enter or leave the ring. We never saw a goddamn punch thrown. All we saw for a 'C Note' was the back of hundreds of ticket holders, who also were pissed off."

My uncle displayed a similar anger when a connected neighborhood "wise guy" disappeared. Tony was an important member of the Genovese crime family, respected, feared, and wealthy by neighborhood standards. My uncle buried Tony's grandparents and parents and obtained the gravesites for the family. The entire family had been a loyal customer over the last thirty years. One day Tony was missing. After more than a month, no one had heard from him. His clothes were still in his apartment, money still in his bank accounts. Without a body, there would be no death notice; without a death notice, there was no need for a gravesite, headstone, casket, funeral parlor, and undertaker. Jimmy shook his head in disbelief. The brown eyes looked up, asking God, "What did I do to deserve not having one of the biggest mob funerals in the neighborhood?"

Jimmy Durante held center stage for Uncle Jimmy on TV on Saturday nights. My uncle never could capture enough, always wanting more. If Durante were on seven nights a week, my uncle would be in his audience. Jimmy was by nature and profession a serious man, but when Durante spoke, my uncle would chuckle then begin to giggle—not laugh but giggle a deep down, inside giggle that would build and build and then explode at a joke or a Durante song. Uncle Jimmy giggled so long and so hard that tears formed in his eyes and his nose started running. Fascinated at the double performance, I laughed until I cried—not at Durante but at Uncle Jimmy. An hour or two after the show, for no apparent reason, my uncle began giggling, the scene replaying itself in his mind—and mine as I repeated my uncontrollable laughter.

Jimmy acquired an old house on acreage in upstate New York about three hours by car from the city. I was a senior, home from college, having just completed ROTC basic training and advanced summer camp. Jimmy asked if I would like to see the place in the country, driving up with him and Phil for the weekend. The three of us got in the dark blue Buick station wagon my uncle used to pick up bodies and transport them to the funeral parlor. Phil drove the first shift; I drove the second. The three of us talked, laughed, and giggled the entire trip.

We arrived at the sixty-year-old house surrounded by dense woods. We unpacked, went on a tour of the small house, and then walked outside for an hour, seeing only trees. We returned to the house, sat on Adirondack chairs on the uncovered large porch, and had a cold beer. Phil took a sip of his drink, stood up, looking at the house then to the woods, and turned to Jimmy. "You know, Jimmy, this would really be a great place if there was like a little park nearby, with a small bench, where you can get away to be with nature."

After much laughter, my uncle asked me for assistance. "I was at the cabin alone, two months ago. I put the garbage in an aluminum can in the screened-in porch outside the kitchen. I went to bed and was awakened during the night by a low growl and the sound of the screen on the porch being ripped. I finally got up enough nerve, went downstairs, and turned on the lights. The garbage can was turned upside down, and trash thrown everywhere."

Jimmy had acquired an M-1 A1 rifle, used in the Korean War, still wrapped in its original packaging, together with a box of several clips of ammo. Since I had successfully completed basic training, Jimmy requested I clean his weapon, zero in and adjust the rifle sights, and teach him how to fire the rifle to defend himself.

I cleaned the rifle, took several clips of ammo, setting up a makeshift bull's eye in a gravel bank in the woods, and began zeroing in the rifle. After I fired the second clip, I felt the weapon was ready for my uncle; calling for him. We went through the safety instructions, then onto holding, loading, bracing, aiming, and firing. After several dry runs, I thought it was time for Jimmy to fire a real round at the bull's eye.

Jimmy stood, braced the rifle butt against his shoulder, aimed at the target, loaded a round, squinted his intelligent brown eyes, and squeezed the trigger, landing him flat on his back. After much laughter, Phil provided these words of encouragement. "You know, Jimmy, if you're going to fire a gun, you should get a good night's sleep the night before, not now." Phil's uncontrollable laughter together with my muted giggles filled the silence.

I picked my uncle up, saying, "Let's do it again. This time, brace the butt into your shoulder and spread your feet wider apart."

Jimmy stood, his dark brown eyes deep in thought. "I'll put the garbage can in the kitchen and leave the porch locked. It will be a lot easier on everyone, including the bear and goddamn Phil."

One night while Jimmy and I were watching a presidential address on television, Jimmy started a conversation on the cold war and Western Europe. I listened for a while then interrupted in mid sentence, making a comment on trade issues across the iron curtain. "What the hell do you know about that?" I told him we had discussed it in class and I read about it in the *Daily News*. He put his hands on the table, leaned over, glaring at me with eyes sparkling, and said, "I asked you, what do you know, not what you read in a newspaper or get from someone's lecture notes. What do you know? How do you know it?" He turned and walked into the kitchen. Of all his comments, that one has stayed with me my entire life.

That evening, we discussed many topics, one of which was attending college. "What do you want to do when you graduate?" That was the first time someone had ever asked me that question, and I had no intelligent, thought-out answer. No one in the family had ever gone to college, but everyone knew a person should attend and graduate. I just had never thought beyond graduation. We continued to watch the presidential address, and being a bit of a "wise ass," I said, "President of the United States."

Jimmy became serious. "Why?"

I began a dissertation on how important the job was, how people would respect me, the power of the position, and the most important reason, "I will be a part of history and always be remembered."

Again, the sparkling eyes, accompanied by the shaking of the head and the raising of the eyes to the heavens, following with the question, "Who was the 21st President of the United States?" I had no idea; I knew who the sixteenth was, so I guessed "Grant".

The head shook, and the smile reappeared. He said, "This isn't twenty questions, so don't guess again. Either you know or you don't. When you guess, you make a bigger fool of yourself." Jimmy's eyes sparkling, he said, "Chester A. Arthur. Chester A. Arthur was one of the least known presidents of the United States, becoming president through the murder of President Garfield. In his almost four years in office, he accomplished very, very little and never sought a second term. So again, why do you want to be president?"

Uncle Jimmy died in the late 1970s. I wish he were alive now so I could thank him for providing the foundation for a happy, realistic life and questions I am still attempting to answer over fifty years later. "What do I know?"

Uncle Joe

Joe Greco eloped with Helen DeVincenzi in the early 1930s; a marriage frowned upon by my grandparents. The DeVincenzi's were from northern Italy outside of Genoa. The Greco family came from Naples, in southern Italy. The Genovese believed they were better than the Neapolitans. The family dispatched my oldest uncle, Albert, and his younger brother, Louie to retrieve the future Mrs. Joseph Greco, but returned empty-handed. The happy marriage lasted until Joe's unexpected death over thirty-five years later.

Uncle Joe had a slender frame, standing five foot eight with a well-muscled physique. He was a semi-professional boxer, played baseball, and used his physical strength at his job, especially during prohibition. He worked for a construction company as a grader operator, constructing highways, airports, and public works projects throughout New York City. Joe took us on Sunday drives to projects he worked on, always proud of his work.

Joe drove a three-wheeled, red motorcycle to work with a storage box behind the seat supported by two wheels. As Joe aged, a Volkswagen Bug became his means of transportation. The first time I saw the car, I gaped in shock—no fins, small, and ugly, like bumper cars at Coney Island. Joe took me for a drive through his neighborhood. Returning home to his driveway, he quickly put the car into the garage. "I always park this ugly red thing in the garage so the neighbors won't see it before dinner and lose their appetites." He shut the garage door, shaking his head. I followed him through the garage to the interior house door, pausing at the tool bench to ogle the calendar photo of Marilyn Monroe.

The man had tremendous energy all the time. I remember as a child the difficulty I had keeping up with him on a walk. Aunt Helen spoke for all of us, asking, "Joe, are you going to a fire? If not, would you slow down so we can all enjoy the walk?"

Uncle Joe and Aunt Helen owned a three-story row house in Ozone Park, Long Island with garden and garage. Visiting their house from Sullivan Street required a three-hour subway and bus ride together with a half-mile walk, naturally carrying two to three shopping bags. We visited mom's favorite sister several times a year during summer and early fall. During my early grade-school years, I spent one or two weeks during summer vacation alone with Aunt Helen and Uncle Joe.

Uncle Joe taught me to play baseball and box when I was six. He gave me one of his cracked leather baseball gloves from the 1920s, taking me to a vacant lot next to the house to play catch with a hardball. In that vacant lot, I learned why it was called a hard ball every time I missed it with my glove.

The vacant lot was next to a grass and dirt baseball field with foul lines, fence, dugout, and bleachers. Neighborhood fans were always present to watch the games. If a game were in progress during our practice, we wandered over to watch the game with Joe analyzing each play, many times predicting the next play. After the game, Joe took me onto the field, letting me play different positions, tossing the ball while describing imaginary situations on the field, telling me how to respond. "Runner on second, one out, slow roller to short." "Good play on the ground ball, but you need to look the player back to second so he doesn't try to sprint to third base; then fire the ball to first." When the field was not in use and no one present, he hit grounders to me with a taped-together, broken wooden bat. Most of the grounders I missed.

Leaving the field and coming back to the house, we changed the game, playing penny ball on the concrete driveway in front of the garage. Joe placed a penny on the driveway and stood opposite me, five to ten feet away. We tossed a rubber ball at the penny. If I hit it, the penny was mine. Over the years, the penny became a nickel, a dime, then a quarter. Joe also increased the degree of difficulty by lengthening the distance between us or having us use our non-dominant hands to toss the ball, even standing on one foot. Joe was good at games, making up ones that were always fun and challenging but never lasting so long that I lost interest.

Baseball continued in his house. Joe was a die-hard fan of the New York Giants, punishing the speaker of the words "Dodgers" or "Yankees" with a stern finger-pointing, angry glance, and English or Italian swear word, no matter the age or gender. Watching National League Baseball, Joe recited the players' batting averages, runs batted in, and the pitchers' earned-run averages. He discussed the team's records against the Giants. Joe knew the players responsible for Giant losses, who received additional attention described in non-flattering terms.

Uncle Joe's most religious experience occurred in 1951. Bobby Thompson of the Giants hit a three-run home run in the ninth inning to beat the Brooklyn Dodgers, sending the Giants to the World Series.

When the Giants and Dodgers moved to California, Joe after all those years had to decide whether to be a fan of the World Champion New York Yankees—to which he replied, "No way in friggin' hell!"—or of a team starting its first season, the New York Mets. He became a Mets fan, accepting Casey Stengel as manager of the Mets, although previously the manager of the hated Yankees. The Mets' losses their first year were a record for any Major League Baseball team, 41 wins 101 losses. Watching the Mets that year was painful, dangerous to your health, even for a twelve year old.

The Mets were playing the Phillies in a doubleheader. We went to the basement of his row house, retrofitted with a kitchen, family room, and bathroom. We ate the lunch Aunt Helen prepared in the family room, remaining fixated on the television screen. The first game of the double header was now in the bottom of the eighth inning, the Phillies ahead by nine runs. Knowing the outcome, Joe shut the television off. We finished lunch and talked about the Mets and the season while anxiously awaiting the next game of the double header. As the time for the second game approached, Joe turned the television back on. Our attention focused on the screen; we listened to every word of the sportscasters. The picture now switched to the Phillies' bullpen. A right-hander was warming up, the starting pitcher for the second game. The Phillie's right-hander had a record of twelve wins and four losses. Although the wins were accomplished prior to mid season, the twelve wins would eventually equate to over 25 percent of the "Amazing Mets" annual record. The camera switched to the Mets' bullpen where two pitchers were warming up a right-hander and a left-hander. The right-hander had a record of one win and nine losses; the left-hander, no wins and seven losses. The announcer fractured the silence, saying, "Casey's decided to play percentages, going with the right-hander." Uncle Joe stood up, shaking his head, shut off the TV, and began a session on dog training, using his constant companion, Trixie, a Boston bull terrier as a pupil, then on to boxing.

My uncle taught me to box at six, teaching hand positions, foot-work, bobbing and weaving, jabbing, punching and counter-punching, always encouraging and rewarding me for attempting these moves. We shadowboxed and sparred, using the rug or the concrete driveway panels as the ring. Typically, I would walk into an open hand and then win the round by Joe awarding me the most points scored for the fight based on the most tears shed.

The tears many times signaled the start of a different game, "Joe's Checkers." Joe used special checkers in the game—chocolate kisses, one side playing with the candy covered in tin foil, the opponent playing with unwrapped kisses. A checker jumped was subsequently consumed; there were no kings. I knew the first move was always desirable, providing a one-move advantage, and I always went first, after many objections by my uncle. The one who made the first move had to use the kisses with the foil removed, while the opponent, Joe, got the checkers covered in tin foil. If I lost a checker, Joe quickly gobbled it up. But if Joe lost a checker, I'd take my time before eating it, concentrating on removing all of the foil because biting into the aluminum wasn't pleasant. During tin foil removal, I lost one or two additional chocolate kisses to Uncle Joe. Maybe going first was not such a good idea!

Uncle Joe's imagination continued even at dinner, with his fork and knife turning mashed potatoes into a series of hills and a roadway covered with brown gravy. Pieces of pot roast became rocks on the hillsides. Broccoli turned upright, inserted in the mashed potato hills, and became trees while carrot cars crammed the gravy roadway.

Helen and Joe lived a half mile from a working dairy farm, and after dinner, we visited the farm. There they introduced me to the most mesmerizing brown eyes, glistening wet noses, and soothing moos of the four-hoofed creatures, which had a smell all their own. We walked down every aisle, observing the rear end of hundreds of cows, all looking terribly the same. Completing our walk and arriving at the house with the sun now setting, I took an old glass jar with a punctured lid to collect lightning bugs, providing an intermittent yellow light that changed my jar into a magic lantern. During the day, I caught grasshoppers and butterflies, none of which lived on Sullivan Street.

Uncle Joe together with brothers-in-law Albert and Louie constructed a garden in the Greco's backyard. They installed a four-foot-high chain-link fence with gate and, within the fenced area, a one-foot-high concrete wall, parallel to the fence and connected to the fence at the gate. Within this enclosed area, plants and flowers filled most of the space but gave room—and cover—for two large snapping turtles, Curley and Larry, and a box turtle named Moe, to "eat the bugs." Lush green grass filled the center of the yard. A one-room, flat-roof, screen structure constructed with two by sixes sat off to one side of the center yard for use in the hot summer nights to keep out the mosquitoes, providing a classroom for extra credit courses in pinochle.

Uncle Joe and Uncle Louie always had dogs. Since neither had children, their dogs became their surrogate pride and joy, causing heated debates on whose dog was the most intelligent. I always loved to be around these dogs; they got into more trouble than I did. When I did get into trouble, which was often, I found a dog to hug, pet, and to give me a tickling lick.

I loved dogs and saw no reason for city living to keep me from having one. My relatives didn't all agree. One time in late November, Mom and I returned from a shopping trip to department stores on

Fourteenth Street off Sixth Avenue. It was cold, and on our way up to Apartment #64, we stopped on the second floor to see my nonna and get warm. Aunts Helen and Nettie were in the apartment, providing warmth of a different sort with kisses, asking questions about our trip. Hugging me, Helen asked, "Did you get to see Santa? What did you ask Santa for?"

"All I asked Santa for was a dog."

Helen was taken aback, saying, "Well if you are good and Santa has enough dogs, you may get one. What else would you ask for if Santa ran out of puppies?"

I never answered the question since I wanted nothing else.

On Christmas morning, Uncles Joe and Louie and Aunts Helen and Nettie came to our apartment to wish us a merry Christmas and present our Christmas presents. Expecting my dog, I was barely able to contain myself and wait to open the big box Uncles Joe and Louie placed on the kitchen linoleum. With sly smiles, they stepped aside, watching me rip off the bow and wrapping paper. Opening the box, I exposed a wind-up metal dog playing drums while moving its head up and down. I hid my eyes, beginning silently to cry.

Uncle Joe came over, picked me up, and said, "Get your coat."

I remember putting on the coat and crying into the woolen sleeve to silence the sobs. Decades later, the distinctive smell of wet salty tears on wool brings back memories of that day. We got into Uncle Joe's Desoto and drove to a pet store on Delancy Street. The store was open. Joe asked the man cleaning out an aquarium, "Your sign says you got everything. Where the hell are your dogs?"

"At the back, down that aisle, in the chrome cage against the wall."

A large cage attached to the rear wall filled with shredded newspaper held mutt puppies, no purebreds. Skippy picked me out, a white lickie puppy with a coffee-can smell. Life did not get better than that for a six year old.

One never knew what to expect from Uncle Joe, although everyone knew it would be fun and laughter. Aunt Helen arranged all family events. Since our family did not have a car; she and Uncle Joe drove us in their Desoto to most events. When I left to go back to college, Helen and Joe drove the family to the airport. Checking in, hands filled with tickets, books, and baggage, after a long tearful goodbye even for our family, I boarded the 4:30 p.m. flight for Seattle.

Sitting in the assigned window seat with a vacant seat next to me, I awaited our departure while anxiously looking out the window for a glance of family. Not being a seasoned traveler and not particularly liking to fly, my mind provided countless scenarios of landing in Seattle, none of them good. Now almost five o'clock, the exit door remained open.

The plane's intercom system buzzed, clicking to life. "This is the captain, and we are experiencing a minor mechanical problem with a sensing light. Takeoff will be briefly delayed."

Maintenance personnel in white jump suits entered, and passengers left the plane to stretch their legs in the terminal. Looking to the aisle, I saw Uncle Joe in brown jacket, tweed pea cap, and unlit cigar clenched between teeth walking down the aisle, staring at everyone and everything around him. "I wonder if Uncle Joe ever flew on an airplane," I thought. But before the almighty responded to my query, Joe was sitting in the vacant seat beside me.

"What the hell is going on? Your mother and father and Helen are outside waiting for you to take off, getting more and more nervous. Are these things always this damn late?"

The captain interrupted our conversation. "We will be departing in approximately sixty minutes. While we are awaiting our departure, we will begin our dinner service."

The flight attendants presented us with menus, and we both ordered steak and wine. We ate our salads, sipped our wine, talked about family, how quickly summer had passed, laughing at the times we had shared. A tray with steak, baked potato, green beans, and another glass of red wine briefly interrupted our conversation. More stories and giggling followed.

"I wonder what the contingent in the terminal is thinking, losing two now to United," I said.

The flight attendant picked up our trays and asked, "Would you like to have coffee or tea?"

Uncle Joe replied with a question. "Do you have any spumoni?"

"We don't have ice cream. Would you like a cookie or an after dinner drink?"

Joe stood up and said, "That's OK. I'm fine, thank you very much." Joe gave me a hug and kiss and then walked off the plane with a smile as wide as the wingspan. The plane took off minutes after Joe's departure. I smiled, silently laughing until landing in Seattle.

Uncle Joe died of a heart attack, one year after retiring while I was away at college. The last time we were together was in New York, on a plane delayed for take off to Seattle.

Uncle Joe taught me how to box, train a dog, play baseball and pinochle. I taught my grandchildren to play penny ball although it's now quarter ball. I enjoy physical activity. I love sports, still playing soccer, learning to play tennis and golf, learning more through losing and trying at times, like Uncle Joe, to do the unexpected.

Aunt Helen, Uncle Joe and me

Sports in the Neighborhood

Sports could turn into tickets to leave the neighborhood, a way to make it in the outside world. Rocky Marciano, boxing heavy weight champion, Joe DiMaggio, Yankee center fielder, Yogi Berra, Yankee catcher, and Willie Pepe, middleweight boxer were role models. How do you succeed without an education? How do you get out of the neighborhood, not in the back of a police car? How do you get a boatload of money? How do you date Marilyn Monroe? You play sports!

We played baseball in the street with traffic, football on asphalt and concrete without pads or helmets, basketball on sidewalks without courts, and street hockey on roller skates with homemade sticks, without helmets or pads. We assembled bikes from bent frames and rusted parts, racing against each other in the streets against traffic with deep religious fervor, assuming the bikes would turn and stop as directed. Most times, they didn't. Neighborhood track and field consisted of two events. All excelled at the hundred-yard dash, escaping the cops, and the high jump, hurtling quickly over warehouse chain-link fences. Form and balance play important roles in every sporting event from wrestling to horseback riding. One of the most difficult gymnastic events in our neighborhood was the Subway Chicken Event, played after an evening of pool.

The gang headed to Chambers Street, which had the only pool hall we could get into at thirteen and was two blocks from the subway station. After playing pool, we took the subway from Chambers Street Station, the end of the line, on a short ride to Canal Street, and from there, we quickly walked to the neighborhood.

At nighttime, the streets and subway were virtually deserted, and local trains, now outside of rush hour, were three cars in length with an operator only in the first car. Once we secured the last car for ourselves, the Subway Chicken Event began. The initiated members of the gymnastic team entered the last car of the train at Chambers Street, making enough noise and raucous behavior that fellow travelers, if any, made their way forward to other cars. The team members then formed a tight circle around the locked rear door with a safety glass window in the top half.

The uninitiated, in this case limited to only one idiot—me—assumed the mount position on the waiting platform. After the doors to the train closed and as the train began moving, the uninitiated jumped onto the last car's outside walkway, a semicircular landing that extended a mere eighteen inches or so past the locked rear door. With no guardrail, the small metal plate offered little for security. Two flimsy chains hung loosely between the four posts attached to the outer edge of the landing, providing some element of safety for those walking from one car to the next. They did little, however, to protect the uninitiated who had to wedge his body between two of the posts.

I knew what to do; I'd had explicit instructions. "Getting onto the landing is safe; don't worry about it. The third rail [which was exposed and provided the electricity to power the subway] is over four feet away. If you fall, just pick yourself up quickly and get back on the platform before the next train comes." No further directions provided.

Once on the platform, having successfully negotiated the posts and chains, the uninitiated stood grasping the metal handles on each side of the locked rear door as the train began to accelerate. Hands now clamped onto the handles in a death grip, with legs violently shaking, knees buckling, and mind filling with fear-consuming thoughts of falling to my death as the train entered the unlit tunnel.

Now came the difficult part for the uninitiated—opening the eyes and demonstrating no fear while glaring at the initiated safely inside the car laughing, forming ugly faces, making lewd gestures with hands and other body parts, and mouthing vulgar phrases. Quickly you silently said any prayer you could remember. Now with some composure, you opened your mouth while screaming and smiling at the same time. The train's speed and the air mass moving behind the train caused your hair to rise, body to shake, the sweat on your forehead to disappear. Unbelievably, body and mind somehow acclimated to the experience; you relaxed the death grip, silenced the scream. Then a train traveling in the opposite direction passed, resurrecting and amplifying fear as screams resumed together with shakes and stuttered prayers.

A purgatorial eternity passed, less than three minutes of time on earth, and the train entered the station at Canal Street. Gymnastic team members' hands stretched out, providing assistance on dismounting. Reaching the station platform, the track and field events began with wobbly legs supporting attempted giant leaps up the station steps onto Canal Street and West Broadway before the tollbooth collector called the cops.

The choice of neighborhood sports depended upon the number of players, the fields available, and the creativity of the participants. Adults never entered into the games—as coaches, referees, or spectators. My parents never watched me play baseball until I was in my mid thirties. Chosen directly after the flip of the coin, you were the first-round draft pick, and you and everyone else knew you were good. If your selection came at the last round or not at all, you got the message and determined what skills you needed to improve if you want to play again. Improving skills took time and effort. Without adults as coaches and their goal of "everyone gets to play," no twenty-four-hour miracles happened in the neighborhood. You needed to prove yourself every day, in every sport. Not selected, being a spectator, hurt. If you wanted to play, you watched, learning the skills needed. Practicing and working to improve, you eventually found that a team chose you in the last round to balance a team, getting the chance to play and prove yourself. Kids were honest without being brutal; tomorrow was a new day and a different sport. Uncle Joe said, "You learn more from losing than winning." I learned a lot.

Kids were managers, coaches, administrators, team doctors, umpires, referees, timekeepers, equipment managers, and statisticians. On several occasions when we needed more players to field teams, we became personal agents to deal with reluctant parents, asking, "Could Vinnie stay down in the street for another hour," or "Edith, we're going to King Street. Can Bobbie come? We need another player." In our world, the flip of the coin decided teams, fair from foul balls, out of bounds, traveling, and penalties. The coin could not be questioned, bullied, or argued with and was as good as it got. Winning was not everything, but on many days, it was close.

The most significant issue in neighborhood sports was the field of play. MacDougal and Houston had the one asphalt field for the entire neighborhood, providing play for football, baseball, basketball, and hockey. Using this field depended upon the older guys not being there. They had exclusive, first-priority rights. If you were one of the younger guys, you got creative in figuring out where else to play. We selected fields based on the day of the week—alternate side of the street parking in effect—closure of a business, and trucks making deliveries. If necessary, we moved cars, pushing, pulling, or jump-starting them to acquire a field of play. We learned to be creative in the game, too, modifying the rules to fit the fields available, rarely choosing the other option—not getting to play.

We had no ice skating rinks in the neighborhood. The only ones were in Central Park, Rockefeller Center, and Madison Square Garden, three rinks for a city with a population of eight million people. So how do you play hockey without ice?

We could only play hockey on weekends when the warehouses and factories closed and then the adjacent streets became our skating rinks. We made goals from two by fours with onion- and potato-sack nets, stored in alleys and cellars when not in use. Rolls of black electrical tape turned into pucks, the street's eight-inch concrete curb with cast iron edge became the boards at the edge of the rink, and a manhole cover in the center of the street the blue line. No one ever called icing, knowing the uncertainty of the call would result in arguments and altercations. Checking opposing players on roller skates against the curb was not a foul but a skill set required of every player. Checking your opponent on roller skates into a no parking sign or fire hydrant rarely resulted in a penalty since the victim quickly got up, determined to get even. We played on.

No salt-water bays or fresh water lakes existed in the neighborhood yet we raced against each other every week in the Sullivan Street Yacht Regatta. We tested our naval, architectural, seamanship, and construction skills in acquiring the materials for our vessels construction. We obtained the beams and planking not from forests or lumberyards but from candy stores. The sidewalks and streets adjacent to candy stores provided the single material needed for vessel construction, the Popsicle stick. To build the ship, we needed a minimum of twelve to fourteen sticks but nothing more. Any glue would disintegrate in the water. The discarded wrappings, although not used for the boat building, gave a special bonus: Twenty wrappers and fifty cents providing admission to the bleachers at Yankee Stadium or the Polo Grounds.

Vessel construction began with the deck by setting three Popsicle sticks parallel and about two inches from each other. We took the others, one by one, and wove them around those three in an alternating fashion. The first one went over, then under, and then over the three; the next one fit right next to that first one and went under, over, and then under them; and so on with the rest of the sticks for the length of the three cross members. Only pressure held the vessel together. Additional sticks became masts for the main sail, rudders, and for artistic embellishment. We raided Mom's ragbag for sails, attaching them to the mast by glue, staples, or twine. Finally, we installed the split-stick mast in the center of the raft, gluing it to the center beam of the hull. The yacht, now complete ready for its maiden voyage, awaited the incoming tide.

Sullivan Street, unlike the rest of the known world, had only one high tide a day, and that on only two days of the week, Tuesdays and Thursdays. Tides on Sullivan Street not related to the orbit of the moon, gravity, or time of day, occurred solely due to the City of New York's

Department of Sanitation street-washing truck. On days of alternate-side-of-the-street parking, the truck discharged its payload under pressure to the curb, water rising and flowing to the nearest storm drain at the corner of Prince and Sullivan.

Like surfers catching a wave, we carefully waited for the breaker, launching our rafts in a race to the drain. Watching the craft navigate the curb, we hoped for smooth sailing. But sometimes a wave broke in front of the raft, slowing its progress, or debris impeded progress, causing second-, third-, or fourth-place finishes. The rafts' speed increased as it approached Prince Street and the vortex formed by the storm drain. Cans, sticks, and debris swirling around the drain now joined by our rafts, making retrieval of individual vessels in the whirlpool challenging for the reflexes in avoiding wet jeans. Most rafts spent Wednesday in dry dock to be sea worthy for Thursday's tide.

We most easily arranged boxing—anywhere, anytime, for any reason. There were always fighters available, with rules known by all—last standing, not crying wins. We boxed in hallways or alleys with the oldest acting as referee. Most matches started with the traditional shaking of the hands, followed with the untraditional sucker punch normally delivered shortly thereafter. Bouts ended with no discernable differences in feelings between winners and losers. The next day, winners and losers joined as teammates in football or baseball, sporting similar black and blue markings and swellings.

Finding a field of play for basketball proved the most difficult. There were only two outside asphalt basketball courts, one on Thompson Street, which we did not control, and one on Houston Street occupied by older guys who played from dawn to dusk. Our games began before or after the older guys, so we learned our craft in the dark with very few fouls called. The tallest player in the neighborhood was five feet eight; guards were five feet or smaller. Dunking only occurred with coffee and doughnuts. Frustrated with waiting for a court, we played basketball on sidewalks, two points for every alternate-side-of-the-street-parking sign you hit. If you were good, you placed the ball between the open space of the last two rungs of the fire escape ladder and won three points and bragging rights. We had no twenty-four-second clock, few fouls, and no technical fouls since there was no foul line to take the shot from and no referees to call one.

Football was not as difficult as basketball to arrange but the most difficult sport to meet players' expectations. We played two-hand touch, four on a side in the middle of Sullivan Street. So what do you do with the other guys? They were the subs, or if eight more showed up, we had two games going at the same time. Having sufficient players for one game with a few extra players allowed substitutions to occur after each play, not because you had to but because you elected to, not wanting any broken bones from disgruntled curb warmers. We became strategists on making substitutions; learning to take advantage of our opponent's weaknesses. We matched speed to no speed, height to no height, weight to too much weight, and smart to not too smart.

We played without pads and helmets, with only a football, the traffic, and us. If the opposing team touched with two hands the player carrying the football, the play was dead. Two hands on the opponent was the equivalent of a tackle. The touches normally came with vigor and maximum force, resulting in many dented car doors and broken antennas. We were out to prove, when given the chance, we could play tackle football.

The football handed to the offensive team after the flip of the coin started the game. The ball's position on the ground separated the teams by approximately three feet, or one giant step. The offensive team hiked the ball; the defense began quickly counting to ten. The offensive team could run or pass, the defensive team crossing the imaginary line of scrimmage only after reaching the count of ten. With cars and trucks parked on both sides of us, we had less than twelve feet of width for play. The goal lines defined by two manhole covers gave us about three hundred feet for the field.

Plays run by the offense were original, conceived by the quarterback, not using Xs or Os but verbal directions: "Count to six, turn right in front of the Manhattan Special truck at the radiator; go," "On four, in front of the green Chevy, come back to the left front fender; go," "On one, I'll run to the fire hydrant, push them toward the Buick; go." Originality occurred when players changed plays as a pedestrian crossed the street or a truck left a parking space, creating downfield blocking and changing a pass play into a running play. We never kicked footballs in the street due to our lack of accuracy and the likely loss of our ball. Instead, the pass replaced the kickoff, and failure in making a first down after three attempts changed possession of the ball at the line of scrimmage. We became competent in passing, but no one in the neighborhood could accurately kick a football. The rare occasions someone attempted the skill only served to remind us why we refrained from it. The few seconds of kicking led, at best, to a boring five minutes of retrieving the football from under a car. Poorly aimed kicks put some footballs into the black hole of Sullivan Street, never to return to their rightful owners.

As a group, we decided to advance our skill set and play tackle football. First, we needed to find a field of play. After much discussion and exploration, we picked a grass and dirt field at Fourth Street Park, Washington Square. We found an open area south of the checker tables on Fourth Street between Sullivan and MacDougal Streets. The field was bordered by a three-pipe rail fence on Fourth Street with a foot-high looped cast-iron border adjacent to the park walkway on the north side, which became the out-of-bounds marker. The field did not form a perfect rectangle, narrowing as it approached MacDougal Street, but we players had comparable imperfections, having no helmets, no pads, no spikes, and no real tackling or blocking skills.

The grass field was heavily used spring through fall, but during winter, with dried brown leaves covering all vestiges of grass, it was normally available for football. We played eight on a side, teams playing both offense and defense. The hitting, tackling, and get-even contact with body-on-body took its toll, even on our young bodies. The most difficult part of tackle football, we all agreed, was the six-block walk back home to Sullivan Street, since the field served not only for playing football but also for walking dogs.

Three major league baseball teams played in New York, the Giants, the Dodgers, and the Yankees. Each of us was a fan of a different team, celebrating every victory, sulking at every defeat. We argued our faith in our team, using batting averages, on-base percentages, runs batted

Father Arthur and the 1957 Football Champions
with Villa Mosconi Restaurant (our baseball right fielder)
in the background.

in, and earned run averages like attorneys before a jury. We studied yesterday's box scores, team standings, team batting averages, and win-loss records, preparing for our daily closing arguments to this jury of our peers. But all our oral statements mattered little in the end; the findings, not disclosed until after the World Series. The World Series championship team became the best team, and that judgment remained until opening day of the next season when we would repeat the whole process. As true and ever hopeful baseball fans, if we didn't have reason to celebrate our team during the off-season, we firmly believed that next year would be different and—our team would win the World Series, and we would be the ones celebrating.

We played many versions of baseball growing up but not until early teens did we get to play real baseball, finally old enough to compete physically for field use. Success in obtaining a field depended upon the number of players, their ages, and their ability to be extremely assertive. The best neighborhood baseball field, on the corner of Houston and MacDougal, had an asphalt surface with an *L* shaped outfield containing a basketball court in center field. This field was home field for all neighborhood teams from ten to thirty years old, for both hardball and softball.

The rules of play required only a slight deviation from the rules of major league baseball—we always had Mosconi as the right fielder. Mosconi played for both teams, never allowing a ball hit his way to escape and always returning it to the infield. Nothing got past Mosconi. A four-story brick row house with a restaurant and bar below, the Villa Mosconi occupied right field, thirty feet beyond second and first base. Ever dependable, always willing to play, Mosconi was our golden-glove right fielder.

Playing on the asphalt surface of the home field required adaptation of equipment as the hard surface wore through the outer leather ball cover. Once the cover had deteriorated, we wrapped and rewrapped adhesive or electrical tape over the ball's core. The ball took on an egg shape, and the slowest groundball became a knuckle ball with home run potential. Fielding a hard hit ball cleanly, that is, with hands as opposed to forehead, chin, or other parts of the anatomy, was a twenty to one shot at best. Crouched, watching the ball rocket to you, not knowing its final alignment or trajectory, took more guts than brains.

Playing on asphalt and concrete surfaces also took a toll on our bodies and our clothes. Slides ripped jeans and caused scrapes, bruises, and stitches for the body parts involved. The surface wore out the toes of our Keds and PF Flyers, remedied by using the same tape used on the ball. Maybe we did have a uniform in the neighborhood but simply didn't know it.

Real baseball with dirt and grass fields, uniforms that matched, and coaches old enough to drive did not come into our lives until high school. Our neighborhood fielded a team with players, from sixteen to twenty-one, playing in the Manhattan Division of the all-city league. At the end of every season, the coach, Johnny Butch, selected three young players from the neighborhood to maintain the team's continuity. He normally picked an outfielder who could hit, a pitcher with a good fastball and an infielder with a glove, which was my job. We neophytes practiced with the team, that first year playing only when games were out of reach and then for an inning or two at most. Butch was a good, generous man, giving of himself to the many teams he coached, taking us to batting cages on Staten Island, spending countless hours teaching and encouraging us for baseball and life.

Our last practice game before the season began was a tradition Johnny had established many years previously. We traveled to Riker's Island, a New York City correctional facility in the East River to play the inmates. We arrived at the main gate, greeted by a correctional facility sergeant, who introduced himself and two other guards. "They will be your guides for the afternoon." He explained the rules of the correctional facility. "You are expected to comply with these rules while at this facility. In addition to following all directions at all times, most important, you are to stay together as a group. If you need to leave the group, to go to the bathroom, you are to ask your guides first, and one of the guides will accompany you."

Laughter followed with a response, "Hey we know how to go to the bathroom. We don't know much, but we do know that."

After another burst of laughter, louder than the first, a different voice spoke up. "We wash our hands. Don't worry about it; we were brought up right. We don't need you guys; we had nuns."

"If you want to go to the bathroom rather than pissing your pants, we will take you there. It would be interesting to see you play our inmates after you've pissed your pants."

I became very attentive, and so did most of the players. After a brief silence some of the older players asked, "Hey, is the new laundry up and running?" "Do you still serve SOS on Wednesdays?" "Movies still play in the gym on Saturday night? If it's a good movie, we might stick around and watch it."

We formed into a single line, walking to a lunchroom adjacent to the prisoners' mess hall for a quick snack before the game. The guards searched our baseball gear for contraband while we ate. Finishing our food, the assistant warden in a suit got up and thanked us for coming, telling us how important this game was for the inmates. He said, "You will be leaving the lunchroom and will walk single file through the prisoners' mess hall to the ball field. You are not to look up, are not to make eye contact with any inmate, and are to stay in line at all times."

We left the lunchroom single file, entering the mess hall. From the back of the line came an observation. "Hey, that's my godfather, Frankie. How yah doing, Frankie?" Portions of the line disappeared into the mass of inmates, many from the neighborhood. Order was quickly restored, and we walked to the ball field.

The sergeant of the guard introduced us to the umpires for the day's game and to the inmate team. We shook hands with the umpires and inmates then headed to our dugout. The umpire in chief came over, asking Butch for his lineup card. Butch took it out of his back pocket, giving it to the umpire. Looking at the card, the umpire began walking back to home plate.

Our shortstop yelled out, "Hey ump, can we get a copy of the inmate team's lineup card?"

The umpire turned to our dugout, laughing. "They don't need a lineup card. I know them all, and they ain't going anywhere without a pardon until after the game."

"That's great if you're a guard, but we still should have a lineup card to follow the game."

"Trust me. I'll let you know if they don't follow their lineup." The umpire in chief began walking back to home plate, suddenly stopped, kicked the nearest mound of dirt, and slowly turning to our dugout, glared. "By the way, son, don't call me guard."

The opposing team, spectators, guards, and the other umpires erupted with laughter. The umpire in chief signaled, "Play ball." Older, bigger, and stronger, the inmates included some outstanding ball players. That inmates served as the umpires had no impact on the game. By the third inning, the game was well out of our reach.

Playing at Riker's Island should have provided us with some insight into our ability and what we needed to do to improve, but sadly it didn't. With our season almost over, our team stood in fourth place. We needed a first or second slot to reach the playoffs. The outcome of the next three games would determine if we still would be in contention for a playoff spot. Losing any of the three games would probably knock us out and eliminate all chances of advancing. We were playing the second-place team in our division, a team that had previously beat us soundly during the first half of the season. The opposing pitcher towered over us at six foot two, a left-hander who threw nothing but fastballs and sliders that we had never hit the last time we had played.

Those factors didn't influence Johnny; he kept his competitive attitude and expected us to do the same. On our way to the field, the older players voiced a little bit of, "I think we know how this is going to end," and Johnny quickly and loudly put that kind of thinking to rest.

By the top of the sixth inning, we were behind by three runs, having hit only two infield singles and three balls out of the infield when Johnny threw in the towel. In frustration, he also threw in a water bottle and then threw two of us "kids" into the game. We managed to escape the top of the inning without giving up a run. We came to bat. After a leadoff walk, the second batter smashed a line drive, one hop, back to the pitcher, rocketing off his left ankle, and down he went. Two coaches assisted the pitcher off the field, and a right-handed pitcher entered the game. The right-hander was not as fast as his predecessor, nor did he have the same control, and we started to play with some confidence. We put together some walks, base hits, and found ourselves behind by only one run with one out and the bases loaded. I came to the plate. During the first half of my brief season, I learned, and Johnny knew, I was not a good hitter, not being able to hit fastballs, sliders, or any other pitch with authority.

Anxiously stepping into the batter's box, I looked to Johnny in the third base coaching box for my sign, anticipating a signal to bunt or take. Looking and not recognizing the sign, I stepped out of the batter's box. Stepping back into the batters box, I looked at Johnny. No sign. Johnny had told us, "When you're not sure of the sign, ask the ump for a time out," so I did. Once time was called, I trotted to the third base coach's box. Johnny was a big guy, and he put his arm around my shoulder, directing me away from third base to the privacy of the left field foul line.

Away from being overheard, I asked, "You want me to take a pitch and try for a walk? You want me to bunt?"

Johnny came to an abrupt halt, looked directly at me, and said, "I want you to get hit with the freakin' pitch."

That was the first time I received career counseling, knowing I would always be buying tickets to any major or minor league baseball game. My shoulder hurt for a week.

Team Photos

Whistle blows, time expires.
Synchronized flash and shutter,
The game remembered forever.

Fingers caress paper edges.
Emotions, details suddenly erupt.
Fields, plays, teammates reappear.

Remembering, so long ago,
Eyes so bright, smiles so large,
Having so little, believing so much.

Spaldeen

When the ice on the Hudson River began to melt, the wind chill diminished, and you could finally feel your fingertips, you knew that spring had arrived on Sullivan Street. Wool gloves and snowballs gave way to leather gloves and baseballs. No packing, no trips to Florida or Arizona, no contracts to sign, spring training began.

Our minor league careers began, not on MacDougal and Houston Street where our neighborhood asphalt ball field was located, but in tenement hallways, alleys, streets, stoops, vacant lots, even rooftops. We played such games as stoop ball, slap ball, punch ball, stick ball, hand ball, off the wall, run down, and penny ball. The ball was not a hardball or softball but a rubber ball. The sound of a rubber ball tossed against a wall in a tenement hallway was as common as footsteps on stairs.

The ball used for these neighborhood games was the "Spaldeen." The Spaldeen was similar in diameter to a tennis ball without the yellow fuzz and ridges. The pink rubber Spaldeen had a dark red line at the diameter where the two halves of the ball were fused. How were these halves joined together, keeping air in its interior providing the ball's bounce? How did the air get inside the ball? Why were new balls covered with talcum powder? The answers to these questions become as elusive as those to "What is original sin and why is it passed on to all of us?" but far more thought-provoking to ten year olds.

For twenty cents, you could go to candy stores like Jake's on Sullivan Street, Sam and Al's on Spring Street, or Pop's on Prince Street and select the Spaldeen of your dreams. Ball selection was both an art and science. The first test was visual inspection—the pinker the color and the greater the amount of talcum powder, the higher the rating. Next, a physical test was conducted: the squeeze. How firm was the Spaldeen? The greater the resistance, the higher the air entrainment and assumed corresponding bounce height. With these criteria satisfied, the final and most significant testing began on the remaining candidates: the bounce test. The intended purchaser carefully grasped a ball in each hand, brought them to eye level, then dropped and caught them. The ball that bounced the highest and maintained its vertical alignment proved the worthy choice. Utilizing identical conditions in all tests took time but ensured purchasing a top quality Spaldeen.

Once at home, we put the Spaldeen to further tests, soaking it to remove all the talcum powder and checking it for imperfections. This final inspection was a waste of time; no one ever returned the ball to the store. Returning a purchase for a refund was a neighborhood taboo; living with imperfections was a way of life.

Each Spaldeen was carefully marked with a ballpoint pen, signifying its rightful owner. Rubbing a Spaldeen with sandpaper or rubbing the ball against a concrete surface could remove all vestiges of ownership and provide salvage rights to the finder. You never had just one Spaldeen in your jeans; you needed two. You carried one old Spaldeen for stickball, where balls were easily lost, and a new ball for stoopball or off the wall, where keeping the ball in possession was easier.

Spaldeen is not a Latin derivative but a neighborhood bastardization of the sports equipment manufacturer Spaulding. Told to get our Spaulding, we would have stood perfectly still, looked at you with a blank stare, and tilted our heads right or left as if you were nuts. Told to get our Spaldeen, we would have leaped up five flights of stairs and been at your side with our Spaldeen before you could have said, "Odds, evens, odds."

Dim lighting, at best, illuminated the tenement hallways, which measured approximately five feet wide by fifteen to twenty feet long. Metal covered the wooden doors; the handrail was wood with cast iron vertical supports, and the steps solid slabs of granite. Two windows occupied each landing together with a single radiator. Within this limited field of play, it was difficult not to hit a metal door or window or run into a hot radiator, the avoidance of each requiring different skills. Accuracy was by far the most important skill to keep the ball in play. An errant ball could find its way down five flights of stairs and involve a long retrieval. Given the opportunity, we always selected playing on a landing closer to the ground floor; even though that placed the game in jeopardy for the building superintendent's apartment was on the bottom floor.

Players required a certain degree of accuracy to hit the ball off the wall to a location where the opponent had a difficult time catching it, resulting in a base hit or a run scored. The ball struck only off the bottom two feet of the wall, which included a six-inch baseboard. Hitting off the wall required the batter to assume a primate's position, swinging his arm with clutched ball in a circular motion, barely keeping the knuckles off the ground. The ball, released on the upward motion, spiraled off the wall. Skilled players placed the ball between the hot radiator and adjacent wall or on the wooden window frame, which sent the ball flying erratically, making it uncatchable and resulting in a hit or run, depending on the day's rules.

Some hall ball players mastered the use of the baseboard. They struck the ball on the outer edge, or point, causing the ball not to spiral but be directed with speed to a difficult location to catch. This required cat-like reflexes from the fielder and knowledge of his surroundings for a hot radiator easily yielded an inside-the-park home run.

The hallways also provided room for slap ball. One and maybe the only fielder pitched the ball on one hop to the batter. The batter used the palm of his hand as a bat to hit the ball. In larger hallways, the batter could run to a base, and if the ball was not caught before he got there, he scored a hit. Handball was also played against the wall, similar to tennis, with the open palm being the racket but no backhands.

Hallway ball taught one speed as well as accuracy. If by mistake you hit an occupied metal apartment door, you ran like hell, descending five flights in record time, before its inhabitant came out and took you by your ear to your family.

As our skills improved and we were allowed to play in the street, our repertoire of games expanded. Stoop ball and off-the-wall now played four to a side between parked cars or relocated cars, on vacant warehouse streets, in the twenty-foot no parking zones around fire hydrants, or at the intersections of two streets. On deserted warehouse streets, weekend teams expanded to five or six players, home plate, and three bases. These vacant streets off West Broadway on Green, Wooster, and Mercer Streets together with Dominic, Vandam, and Charlton off of 6th Avenue were highly prized as stickball fields.

Stickball was for us pure baseball—a pitcher, batter, catcher, one or two bases or manhole covers, an infielder, and if played in the center of the street, an outfielder. The skilled pitchers threw curves, sliders, fastballs, knuckleballs, and the infamous spitter. To succeed at stickball, a batter required cat-like reflexes, instinctive eye-hand coordination, and excellent eyesight, including night vision. Not hitting the ball on the sweet spot resulted in a pop up or groundout at best; at worst, a foul ball and lost Spaldeen. Playing in traffic or at night by light from street lamps further complicated the game. Seeing gave way to guessing, and mistakes caused angry car owners who, upon finding scratches and bent radio antennas, went searching for the culprits.

Many older Italian women stooped over when walking to and from the stores and churches in the neighborhood, the stoop diagnosed by many as osteoporosis. The experienced neighborhood resident knew better; the obvious cause was stickball. Every broomstick and mop stick in the neighborhood had been cut down to provide the Louisville Slugger of the batters dreams.

A block of tenements would furnish three to four baseball teams daily, from sunrise until sunset. We played beyond sunset, relocating the field of play to locations near street lamps. Competition was fierce among us and other neighborhood blocks fielding teams. We didn't need Santa to tell us; we knew who was good and who was bad.

During the baseball season, teams made challenges, "neighborhood style," to those from another block. First, we selected the game format—stick ball, stoop ball, or off the wall. Next, we determined the playing fields, one on each team's block. Then we got down to the details—the rules of play for each of the fields selected, the times for the games, and the amounts bet.

Our Sullivan Street field was a vacant lot between two tenements, 119 and 125 Sullivan Street. The lot had once housed a two-story, brick, truck garage. Approximately eighty feet long and fifty feet wide, the field had enough space for off the wall and stickball. Protruding concrete, brick, broken glass, and rubbish littered the surface, so we swept, raked, and picked up before each game, placing the bases, flour foul lines, and batter's box.

We explained the ground rules to all members of the visiting team from Thompson Street—the strike zone painted on the wall behind home plate for stickball and the penalty line for off the wall. Our field had only first and third bases, each pieces of linoleum, and a cardboard pentagon served as home plate. The outfield-building wall had an additional brick wall, which ended approximately twenty feet off the ground that supported the roof of the former garage. This ledge was in play and any ball off it was playable. If the ball was caught off the wall before it hit the ground, you were out; if not, your fate was determined on the base paths.

Right field provided the greatest challenge and the most rule explanations. The easterly fifteen feet of the playing field indented at forty-five degrees to the vertical wall. The indentation of the building originally bordered the airshaft located between it and the torn-down truck garage. The ground elevation changed at the airshaft, being a foot and a half lower than the main field. The drop in elevation and angle of the brick wall made this a most difficult challenge for any outfielder attempting to catch the ball off the walls. The situation was made even more complex due to the presence of a dry cleaning establishment on the ground floor of 125 Sullivan Street. "Dick the Tailor" had been here for years, and his clothes press steam line exhaust entered the airshaft at exactly the center of the right field playing area. Two-hundred-degree steam discharged erratically, without warning, making playing right field, playing in hell.

We never lost a game to any team on our field thanks to Petey D. Petey D played right field like Willie Mays played the Polo Grounds and Mickey Mantle played Yankee Stadium. He knew every angle a Spaldeen would take if it hit the forty-five-degree wall or the vertical wall and the windows with their metal bars and grates. Most important, Petey D knew that from the interval the press released a swish to the time the steam discharged was seven seconds, enough time to decide your leap or to play the ball off the wall. We all watched Petey D in awe as we watched Fred Astaire dance with his broomstick or Gene Kelley his umbrella. Petey D's play took on the elegance of a work of art. Rather than a physical threat to Petey D, the steam press turned into an object around which to choreograph his leaps.

Improvisation, creativity, knowing your ability, operating as a team member, working to succeed, using what was available, and playing right field in Hell's Bleachers helped prepare us for life.

Social Athletic Clubs (SACs)

Older guys in the neighborhood hung out in cafés, bars, and restaurants, places to meet and visit friends, share laughs, and avoid an honest day's work. The hangout became your second home and family, a lot tougher than Mom and Dad but still family. Unfortunately, it took a lot of cash to spend time in bars, cafés, and restaurants. Time we had; a lot of cash we did not. We became members of social athletic clubs (SACs).

Every city, town, and unincorporated community throughout the United States has a golf club, tennis club, yacht club, hunt club, or organization of some sort to draw like-minded people together. Some clubs revolve around non-athletic endeavors, based on a connection to colleges, political orientation, nationalities, or religious beliefs. To become a member of a club required a sponsor and a lot of cash, which if you had you would not need to be a club member. We possessed none of these elements, so we started our own club.

The City of New York issued charters for social athletic clubs with the stipulation that founding members be of legal age to vote, pay the appropriate licensing fee, and submit a club name. In the middle of the Italian South Village, thanks to a high school French class member with a D minus, the Chateau Social Athletic Club became a reality, located in a former mattress shop, a storefront in 107 Sullivan Street.

The first honorary members were the two older brothers of legal age who signed the storefront lease and applied for the charter and license. Club members were the fifteen- and sixteen-year-old guys who came up with twenty bucks each to pay for the charter, license, two months' rent, and fifteen third-hand folding chairs, two apple-crate tables, several decks of cards, and a radio.

The storefront with drab green peeling paint on its walls, brown rust ceiling, four sixty-watt ceiling lights, and a mop sink hardly fit the definition of plush. The former tenant, the mattress maker, lived in the tenement building, using the interior door from the storefront to the tenement hallway to access the stairway to his apartment for lunch and bathroom use. As the first month ended, we held our first chartered meeting, electing our first club officers and unanimously deciding our first order of work, to construct a bathroom. No one had any knowledge of how to accomplish this task so we did what we always did: We began the neighborhood inquisition. "Who knows anything about building a bathroom?" We sought advice from anyone, guys who did some kind of plumbing work or knew others who did. We spoke to neighborhood janitors, carpenters, and electricians. We borrowed tools, purchased equipment and materials, and debated bathroom layout, methods of construction, flooring types, lighting location, paint colors, even toilet paper holders. Every debate resulted in a show of hands, followed by a show of fists with discussions and altercations blended into our world.

Completing the bathroom using borrowed tools but our own swear words, we next focused our attention on the construction of a bar with a sink and a beer refrigerator to test the bathroom's capability. We redid the floors, repainted the walls and ceiling, installed subdued lighting, and purchased secondhand tables and a TV set. We negotiated with the Genovese family's Mafioso capo, for leasing a jukebox for the club. Negotiated might not properly describe a discussion between two sixteen-year-olds and a Mafioso capo and his brother, but we did get what we wanted—a jukebox that provided music for dances, as well as additional revenue for the club and the local Mafioso lieutenant.

The club sponsored dances on Saturday nights with tickets sold for drinks at the bar. The Chateau, in keeping with the language of its charter, also sponsored club sports, baseball and basketball, and gin and poker games. The place always had some activity going on—a sports game on TV, a card game in progress, a record playing on the jukebox. Family members, neighborhood visitors, old and young, guys from other clubs, everyone felt welcomed and hung out at the Chateau SAC.

Another visitor to the Chateau SAC from the 22nd Precinct was "Paul the Cop." Paul's job was to keep track of us, making sure our activities were reasonably lawful. On a Friday night or weekend night, Paul, dressed in khaki pants and a V-neck sweater over a tee shirt, knocked on the door to the Chateau SAC.

"Who the hell's there?"

"Hey, it's me, Paul."

"Is it Pauli, or is it Paul the cop?"

A smiling face poked through the open street door. "It's me, Paul the cop. You guys blew my cover."

"How yah doing, Paul? We thought you were going to work day shift to help out with the kids. What are you doing here?"

"I'll tell yah what he's doin' here. He's gonna break our chops. We can't get rid of him; we may as well charge him dues. Sit down have a soda. We got any more salami and cheese for Paul? Good, get off your butt and get him some."

"A soda is great. Don't need any more food. What you guys been up to?"

"Nothing!" we said, smiling in unison."

"I know a fairy tale when I hear one." Sipping his soda, Paul sat down at the card table to play a game of gin solely for sport since he was on duty. Paul used the game to ascertain our current behavior, hints on future behavior, and potential problems. We got to know Paul, having many personal discussions on many different subjects over gin games.

We were card players, focusing on the cards discarded, cards remaining, changing our hand accordingly. Paul focused on us, making mental notes to become words and sentences in his report to the 22nd Precinct. Paul knew us better than we knew each other. On occasion, Paul advised us to stay away from certain neighborhood places, streets where activities were going down, other places to avoid to stay out of trouble. We liked Paul. We trusted him, and I think he trusted us.

We were good kids but not that good. At a Saturday night dance at the Chateau, the jukebox blaring in the background, dancers on the black and white linoleum tile floor, and drinks and discussions at the bar, most couldn't hear the disagreement and eventual altercation that erupted outside the club. Although those inside the club didn't hear the noise, outside at one in the morning, neighbors around it did and placed calls to the 22nd Precinct. A black and white was immediately dispatched to 107 Sullivan Street. The flashing lights against the black backdrop and the shrill siren heard above their arguments persuaded the participants in the altercation to stop the match and return to their neutral corners.

Running into the club, Joey reached behind the jukebox and pulled its plug out of the electrical socket. Ronnie turned out the lights, telling everyone, "Shut the hell up!" Mike "Smash" opened the door to the tenement hallway and commanded, "Follow me up to my grandmother's apartment and keep quiet now." We quickly exited the club, locking the door and following Mike up to his eighty-year-old grandmother, who was the superintendent of the tenement, her apartment directly above the club. Mike knocked on the door. "Nonna, it's me, Michael."

Carefully the door opened, revealing Lucretz in a nightgown, bathrobe, and shawl. "Michael, it's one thirty in the morning. What do you want?"

"Nonna, we need to stay here for a while until the cops leave."

"This time only, never again, and be quiet."

Outwitting the cops in our neighborhood was like beating the Yankees in the World Series. Twenty-something of us entered the dark three-room apartment, standing skirt butt to belt buckle, the silence interrupted by Lucretz's mantra, "What, dear God, did I do to deserve this? Tomorrow, Michael, I will tell your mother; your father will beat the holy Be Jesus out of you. Tell your friends to be quiet and not wake up the tenants, and don't touch anything."

An almost undetectable giggle infectiously passed through the apartment, oblivious to "Smash's" grandmother. We stood quite still although some of us continued applying ice to wounds acquired during the altercation. The siren and flashing lights of the black and white stopping directly below us suddenly silenced the giggle. The patrol cars' doors opened and slammed shut, flashing red lights intermittently illuminating the dark green bedroom walls.

"The door to the damn club is locked. Give me the flashlight. I'll climb onto the concrete handrail support and look inside." On the top of the concrete wall, the police officer looked above the green painted storefront window into the top three feet of clear glass required by city code.

"Nobody's inside; the joint's deserted."

"Get off the wall. Let's take a drive up to Bleecker then down Thompson to Grand and see if we can pickup any stragglers."

The flashing lights were extinguished, and the engine slowly accelerated up Sullivan Street, our cue, quickly sending us out by twos and threes from "Smash's" grandmother's apartment.

The next day, Sunday, found the club unusually quiet, no softball games, sports or poker challenges. Sunday night showed more of the same, three of us playing ten-card gin, instead of seven-card, extending the time of the game, and making the lonely night shorter.

Father Arthur, the pastor of Saint Anthony's Church, knocked and, not waiting for a reply, stuck his head through the door, not requiring an introduction. Individually gathering our composure, we welcomed him, offering appropriate drink and food. Father sat down at the card table with his glass of ginger ale. We waited. Father visited infrequently and without warning, coming solely for special needs or problems in the neighborhood. We knew we had a problem.

Father Arthur was intelligent, articulate, sensitive to people's needs, and conversant in many subjects, including sports. Visits with the guys invariably began with a discussion of current sports events, this being Father Arthur's Epistle to the Philistines. Finishing his ginger ale at the poker table pulpit, he prepared to deliver the gospel during our choice of a game of gin, poker, or blackjack. We decided on seven-card gin, and Father joined to make it a foursome.

The dealer distributed the seventh cards, and the players reached for theirs, filling out and arranging their hands. Father Arthur picked up all seven cards at once, never glancing at a single one. With hands over his unexposed seven cards, he broke the silence. "I heard about last night. You guys need to know the 22nd knows you guys were involved."

"Whoa, Father, not us; you got it wrong."

"We ain't done anything."

Father quickly put on the table his seven cards, blind side up, and his hands on top of the cards while glaring at us. Silence. Eyes attempted to avoid contact with the priest's. We squirmed in our confessional mode, no wise remarks and no jokes, faced with a religious dilemma—to squeal on each other or lie to a priest. This was a person we knew, a man who trusted us, a giving and caring priest who eventually heard our confessions. Lying to a priest face to face counted as a sin far greater than mortal and would surely result in excommunication and a ticket for all eternity in hell.

"Yah know, thinking about it, it could have been us."

"We were outside the club last night; it was warm."

"We were minding our own business."

"We didn't start it."

Father stood up, staring, not saying a word, letting our words sink into our hollow heads. We had squealed on each other as well as on those not present, and our fate now rested completely in his hands.

"If any of you guys ever get caught doing anything like this again, the 22nd will throw the book at you, and no one will be able to pull your butts out of the fire. Let's play gin!"

With a silent prayer of thanks, we arranged our hands again, changing our strategy, knowing our luck was not enough now to draw to an inside straight. Petey D won the first game; Rocco, the second.

Father looked at his watch. "Time for one more game. I'll ante up five bucks; you guys put up nothing. If I lose you each get five bucks. If I win you owe me a favor."

Each of us knew he had us. He always won these games, costing us volunteer time at the church, a donation of time or money to a family in need. We sat quietly, knowing the eventual outcome although having no idea of the specifics.

"Is the Big Guy upstairs looking over our shoulders and ratting on us to Father Arthur?"

"How the hell do you hide your cards from God?"

"I'll bet the Big Guy and Father talk to each other during the game. They do that all day long. For them it's not even a miracle. A piece of cake is what it is."

"I wonder what the hell this is going to cost us."

The three of us enjoyed the late cold breakfast after helping to serve the hot breakfast, clean up, and wash dishes after the nine o'clock mass for the Holy Name Society. This gin game had less impact on my life than Father Arthur's twenty bucks I bet against and lost. I became an unwilling actor in a neighborhood play. We rehearsed twice a week for three months at Saint Anthony's memorial hall, on nights bingo wasn't scheduled. Finally *Charley's Aunt* opened, playing to family and friends for four nights. I played the role of Lord Fancourt Babberly, a.k.a Charley's Aunt, and I felt I lost significantly more than the twenty bucks I had bet against.

The Chateau SAC kept us together growing up and keeps us together still. Annual reunions keep alive and well the relationships that started over fifty years ago.

Inside the Chateau Social Athletic Club

The author as Charley's aunt

Aunt Helen, the "Head Aunt"

Helen nurtured and directed the DeVincenzi family for sixty years. In Italy, she had worked with Nonna, tending goats, sheep, and chickens, cooking, cleaning, and growing vegetables, and as the youngest female, sleeping with her mother. At seven, she saw her father leave Italy for America. Six years later, no longer the child, Helen gave directions to other family members while looking to her mother for approval as she helped the family prepare for their journey to America and anticipated reunion with their father. Helen's world drastically changed when she boarded the passenger ship at La Spezia, spending a month steaming toward New York City. The world the family knew, the tranquil, small farming village in the hills above Genoa, was about to change into the noisy, massive New York City. The tenements, cobblestone streets, and hordes of buses and cabs replaced the wooded hills, dirt roads, and flocks of sheep and goats.

The family left Italy with hope and fear of the future, believing family and their religion the only tools necessary for success. How do you succeed, how do you feed your family, having no skills, no money, and no ability to speak and understand the language of this strange land? At Ellis Island, they were met with long lines, questions they didn't understand, and confusing directions, quickly turning the family's hope into fear.

Helen, in a male-dominated society, with little formal education but with self-confidence and self-determination, became the family spokesperson. From that point on, if my grandparents became confused or could not deal with questions, if any member of the family doubted a response, they knew the solution: "Get Helen; she will know what to do."

Animated voice, hand signals, and the two words of English she picked up yesterday, placed her in the family's leadership role. She dealt with the directions, the filling out of forms, and the ridiculous questions. "Why did you and your family come here?" Helen responded, "To eat."

Helen became, in a vacuum, the DeVincenzi spokesperson, directing the family with bags and packages from Ellis Island to New York City. The gray ferry with crew in gray uniforms left Ellis Island, and within an hour, the family saw their new home, the city streets, and the buildings colored the same as the ferry and its crew. Approaching the terminal, Helen recognized her father in a swarm of anxious spectators, awaiting the ferry's arrival, and she led the family into his arms for hugs and kisses.

Upon arrival, Helen obtained a job working in one of the sweatshops bordering the neighborhood, sewing women's clothing. After only a few months, she managed to obtain jobs for family members and friends. Helen demanded all show up at work every day, be reliable and trustworthy, and always perform exceptional work. "If you don't work hard and do good work, I'll tell them to fire you." After dinner at the kitchen table, she set out piecework for the women, earning additional money off the books by sewing undergarments or making artificial flowers, each piece subject to Helen's approval. Afterwards, she pooled the earnings, delineated family priorities, and distributed the money. If you questioned the outcome, you spoke to Helen. She listened, and in turn, she questioned, showing understanding and respect and, on rare occasions, modifying the distribution. Whatever the decision, Helen made "all in the best interest of the family for the future."

After a few months, others sought Helen's guidance, even for day-to-day issues, sometimes receiving a bonus of her unsolicited advice. Helen accepted the leadership role of the family, understanding she was making decisions that affected future generations. Self-confident, street-smart, and capable in her role, she recognized her abilities together with her weaknesses. The family always came before individual needs, including Helen's. The Head Aunt led by example. "Family always comes first!" Few challenged her commandments, everyone wanting to get to heaven, rather than suffering hell on earth. Helen trusted her judgment without second-guessing, and her mission became ours. "We will succeed so our children and grandchildren will have better lives."

Helen made her mother's and father's lives better every day, but her role at Christmas exceeded their dreams. The DeVincenzi family left in Italy close relatives and friends. Without the ability to read and write, they could not correspond, and their only knowledge of the family came from stories told by recent immigrants. At Christmas time, Helen hired a woman from the neighborhood who was literate in Italian, the Genovese dialect, and English to compose with family the "Christmas Letter."

Thirteen adults and I gathered around the kitchen table in Apartment #32, overflowing into the pantry and living room. The Head Aunt introduced the scribe and announced to the family the letter's recipient and address. The scribe began writing nodding in concurrence; everyone now echoed his or her concurrence, "Bravo, Bravo!"

The family asked Nonno to begin the letter to his family in Italy. My grandfather stood, proud, back straight. Minutes passed only silence. A smile emerged under pink cheeks and wet eyes, and he said, "*Bon Natale per cent' anni* (Merry Christmas for a hundred years)." He quickly sat down to applause and imaginary kisses thrown from the lips of the audience. Now Dominica took her turn to add to the letter. She stood up, cheeks red, eyes closed, not saying a word, and quickly sat down, burying her face in her hands. After repeated requests, my nonna shook her head, declining to add to the letter. After hugs and kisses to their mother, sentences and paragraphs loudly flowed and overlapped from family members.

"Ask Silvio if he had a bambino."

"Did they get our last package?"

"We saw Maria yesterday, Tommaso's aunt. She said to say Bon Natale."

"Is it cold yet?"

"Who left the village last year?"

"Take some of the money we send and light Christmas candles for the dead; our prayers will be with yours."

Aunt Helen finally restored calm, giving her mother a kiss, then pronounced the order to follow for providing comments for the letter. Upon completion, each family member received the letter for review and approval—although none of the family could read or write Italian—gave a thoughtful glance, a smile, bowed the head in concurrence, and then passed it on. After all had had a chance to look it over, the letter returned to the scribe for postage. Helen paid her fee, and then coffee, pastries, anisette, and red wine to celebrate.

Helen was the obedient daughter, sewing women's lingerie with her sisters in sweatshops, helping her family financially when anyone needed help, cleaning, repairing, painting apartments, and the common hallways of 120 Sullivan Street, always there, providing help, advice, and support to family and friends. Then something changed. She no longer completely obeyed her mother and father; sometimes, she was unavailable to family members for advice and assistance. Joe Greco had entered her life. She loved the man, from the "wrong" part of Italy, against the wishes of her family. She eloped before her older brother Albert and younger brother Louie could find her and bring her home. "How could a lovely young lady from Genoa marry this person from, of all places, Naples? This is a family disgrace, a northern Italian marrying a southern Italian. How could this happen? Dear Lord, what did we do to deserve this? Why does she hate us so?"

Helen achieved independence, moving to Long Island with Joe, gradually assuming the role of Head Aunt for the Grecos. Over time, the wounds healed, and Helen reassumed her role as advisor to the DeVincenzi family, sacrificing at times her relationship with her husband to attend to the needs of her birth family. Aunt Helen was a mind reader, recognizing needs and providing support and comfort before the family member recognized having those needs.

Aunt Helen preferred to work behind the curtain, maintaining confidentiality, although sometimes she had to step in front. If there was a birthday or anniversary, she worked to ensure there would be a party, a place reserved, and someone to sponsor the event. Everyone knew who had to bring what and, if necessary, who had to provide transportation. It was no easy feat to have fifty to sixty family members at the same place at the same time with agreeable dispositions.

Aunt Helen dealt with difficult family issues, advising family members to seek employment, decrease the amount they drank or the sums gambled, respect and honor relationships with spouses. The messages delivered head-on insured that the subject could not say, "I don't understand what the hell she meant." She presented guidance in a similar manner to all family members with respect, understanding, and love. You listened and changed, no other options provided.

"Respect your family; before you leave your spouse, it's important you clean up your mess before you start another one."

"Don't take yourself too seriously; you'll be disappointed in the end. Just be happy."

"Respect others; don't criticize or laugh at them. He who laughs last, laughs best."

Aunt Helen and Spike Lee shared a quote, "Do the right thing; it matters."

When Aunt Mamie was in her four-year battle with an aggressive cancer, it was Helen, living the farthest away, who took her to doctor's appointments and hospitals for surgeries, staying with her in hospital rooms, and visited daily. She spent nights away from her husband, sleeping on her mother's couch near her younger sister, providing help as needed and someone to cry with. All the brothers and sisters came to support their younger sister and parents. Despite the hard time, Apartment #32 always overflowed with caring, happy people who truly loved each other. When Aunt Mamie passed away, Helen arranged a support group for my grandparents, using family, friends, and neighbors to make sure her mom and dad were taken care of. As I walked through the neighborhood, people whose faces I recognized but whose names I remembered not said, "Hey, I spoke to your Aunt Helen yesterday." She took on this role and willingly played it until her death, even beyond. Before she died, she participated in her own funeral, directing the undertaker and making all the arrangements for her final ceremony to minimize the family's sorrow.

Aunt Helen had no children, so my cousins and I became her children, and she became my Understudy Mother. Helen never missed sending a card for a birthday, anniversary, graduation, or holiday and sometimes just because she wanted to. Many newspaper correspondents have a byline, phrase, or sentence that distinguishes them from others. Helen had one of her own, "Love you very much. What do you need?"

After I outgrew my homesick phase, Aunt Helen took me for visits to her house. I spent weeks in summer and Easter vacation with Helen and Joe, and my aunt and uncle came to visit my grandparents two to three times a month, so we got to know each other quite well. Their house in Ozone Park was very different from Apartment #64. Their house had a yard with grass and vegetable and flower gardens. Inside the house, they had the latest technology—radios, two TVs, two telephones, and a toaster! I drove my aunt crazy. I had toast in the morning, toast for my sandwich at lunch, and toasted sliced Italian bread at supper, much to Uncle Joe's displeasure.

After breakfast, I got to do something I had never done before. I watched *Ernie Kovac's Morning Show*, wild, weird, and quite different from other shows. I loved it. Helen cared little for the show and the humor displayed, and I heard her saying in the background, "That is so stupid. You keep on watching this, you're going to be stupid too." She let me watch the show anyway, sitting and laughing at times with me, sometimes discussing the humor of the Nairobi Trio.

Their place always offered something to do—weed the garden, paint the fence and handrails, walk to the dairy and the grocery store. On such walks, our last stop before the ice cream store was always the butcher shop owned by Uncle Joe's nephews. Helen shared family stories with her nephews and then followed with comments of how tough and fatty last night's meat was. After a brief pause, laughing and running behind the counter to give a hug to the closest nephew, she would place her order for the next day and pick up today's. We always walked a different way back to her house as she introduced me to new

Aunt Helen and me

parks, neighborhoods, schools, churches, and stores, stopping at one or two. Aunt Helen loved flowers, and on our walks, she pointed to them, telling me their names in English and Italian, as her father did in the vacant lot adjacent to 120 Sullivan Street.

After dinner, Uncle Joe and Aunt Helen sometimes took the car out of the garage, and we would head off to an amusement park, a miniature golf course, a walk along the boardwalk, the racetrack, or the trotters. The longer I stayed, the more I understood the depth of my aunt's love. One morning after breakfast, I told her how my dad had taken me to Central Park, and with a safety pin, some thread, and Wonder bread, I had caught a sunfish. It was the first fish I ever caught.

Two days and two bus transfers later, we arrived at Great South Bay with Uncle Joe's old fishing rod. We looked for bait and, with local advice, found ugly reddish brown centipedes, four or five inches long with hundreds of legs, under rocks at the shoreline. Aunt Helen took one and baited the hook, which I tossed over the edge of the dock and caught my first perch. Aunt Helen, the Head Aunt, dignified, self-confident, a proud, lovely woman, was baiting hooks and clapping with joy when a perch hit the wooden planking of the pier. She cleaned and cooked that day's catch of three perch for dinner.

Pat and I married in Seattle while I was still in the Army, having just returned from a year in Southeast Asia. We had a small ceremony with few of my relatives in attendance. My folks who were uncomfortable traveling to Long Island by subway considered Seattle another universe. But Aunt Helen made sure they made our wedding, accompanying my parents on a train trip across the country in mid January (my folks did not believe in flying). Once they had arrived, we introduced them to groups of non-Italians, different cultures, foreign foods. No longer in control of their everyday needs, my parents turned once again to Helen, the translator, who bridged the gap.

Eighteen months later, Pat and I arrived in New York with the first grandchild, our daughter Laura. Aunt Helen gathered the troops at the airport—Aunt Nettie, Uncle Louie, and the proud grandparents—to greet us and welcome the new arrival to the family. We rarely held our daughter during that week in New York; a helping hand, with a flashbulb in the background, always seemed to come out of nowhere to hold the newest member of the family. Helen helped Mom prepare the apartment, rent the crib and highchair, and schedule a party in Staten Island for the whole family to meet this "Wonderful Gift," Laura. The birth of a new family member was a special time for celebration. Aunts, uncles, cousins, and friends made us feel so lucky and proud of our daughter. The family treasured our other children, Joe and Annemarie, with similar outbursts of joy and love in later years, making each feel loved and special. Aunt Helen took the relationship a notch higher, considering all children royalty. She treated us superbly, meeting all our needs whether spoken or not and exceeding all expectations.

Peekaboo

"Peekaboo, I see you."
Moving hands from eyes,
You smile, covering eyes,
Fingers wide, not trusting surprise,
Laughing, giggling, in anticipation.

"Peek boo," you exclaim,
Hands moving from eyes,
Giggling, laughing. "Again."
First thing in the morning, last thing at night,
A game of sheer delight.

"I see you," I say,
Closing eyes, counting to ten, searching
In closet, behind couch, under chair,
Counting to ten, again and again.
"I seek, you hide." "Peekaboo."

"I see you," first day of school,
Running to bus, swinging pack, looking back.

Off to college, away from home,
Majors, minors on your own.
Beginning your dream.

"I see you," leaving for an interview,
Strolling, swaying purse, looking back.
Walking down the aisle,
Driving away, not looking back.
Moving hands from my wet eyes.

"I see you," sitting with your child,
Moving hands from your eyes,
Pulling them aside with complete surprise,
Laughing, giggling, saying
"Peekaboo, I see you."

A short time after returning to Seattle, placed on orders, I returned overseas. Mail call in Vietnam for me was once a week, receiving several letters from Pat, one from Mom, and one from Aunt Helen. All of Helen's letters ended with the same words I had received on her cards growing up, "I love you very much. What do you need? She added a postscript, "Be a good boy." Reading those words, I laughed, wondering what my aunt thought being a good boy meant fighting a war in Vietnam.

I returned home, discharged from the army, found a job, and acquired a mortgage, as well as a son and another daughter. My folks unexpectedly announced they were coming out for a visit. Aunt Helen accompanied my parents together with cousins Jimmy and Gilda, driving their car to Seattle. I had just started my new civilian job, and with Pat at home with the kids, we had no reserve funds. But I knew what we had to do. I looked at the cabinets and pantry and told Pat, "We really need to go grocery shopping."

Pat asked, "Why? I shopped yesterday."

I explained, "My family wants to make sure they never again suffer as they did from the hunger in Italy and during the Depression. For them, that means making sure their pantry and cabinets are always filled with food. And ours too."

Pat returned to the supermarket and stacked the shelves with cans of tomatoes, boxes of pasta, jars of roasted peppers and an extra gallon of olive oil and jars of black and green olives some with pimentos. The day after their arrival, Mom, Aunt Helen, and cousin Gilda began the General Inspection. They casually walked into the kitchen. Gilda, commenting on the size of the pantry, opened its door. Helen smiled, looked at Mom, and said, "Vera, look at all the food." Mom smiled, looking at Pat and me, and I relaxed. We had passed inspection.

Gilda and Jimmy left by car to visit a cousin in California. Aunt Helen, Mom, and Dad would take a train back to New York, now experienced travelers. Unbeknown to us the Head Aunt had invited two younger cousins, Diane and Lisa, to spend a week at our house. We took the ten-person group sightseeing in Seattle and on day trips to the mountains and ocean. One memorable afternoon, after having watched an inspiring Three Stooges movie the night before, we decided to have a whipped cream fight. We made our pies by spraying whipping cream onto paper plates. Each plate was filled with whipped cream until the cream covered the edges of the plate. My cousins, our children, Pat, I, and even our dog faced off. Aunt Helen blew a whistle, and the battle was on. Helen watched this event, laughing and shaking her head, together with my parents. Unable to resist, Helen picked up a paper plate with whipped cream, came from behind, and covered my face with white foam, laughing, shrieking, and twirling with her hands high in the air. The victim laughed with the Head Aunt, not daring to reciprocate.

When my folks and Aunt Helen came to our house, we never knew how long they would stay but it was always a minimum of six weeks. We had tight quarters inside as well as out with three children, five adults, a dog, three cats, several kittens, a goat, two sheep, three geese, a pony, pigeons, and chickens. Mom and Dad slept on a sleeper couch, and Aunt Helen on a bed we rented for the visit. Sharing two bathrooms and sleeping space, all with a minimum of privacy for over two months, testified to their desire to be with their grandchildren. Aunt Helen was in summer camp, never saying a negative word, smiling, maybe remembering the farm in Italy.

Aunt Helen and Uncle Joe's one and only house, purchased in the forties, had three stories. The bottom was the garage, family room, partial kitchen, and bathroom, and the top floor was a rental. Helen and Joe lived on the second floor, which consisted of a bedroom, living room, dining room, kitchen with a little breakfast nook, and a bathroom. Both could always be found in the kitchen and the family room downstairs. When I visited growing up, I stayed on the first floor. I remember climbing the stairs and entering these second-floor rooms once or twice, only on very special occasions. In the mid 1990s, Pat and I visited Dad on an extended weekend, landing at Kennedy. We asked Helen if we could visit her on our way into the city. With our flight scheduled to arrive at 8:30 p.m., we would spend the night at Aunt Helen's, then head to the city the next day. Fog in Seattle delayed takeoff, and we didn't land until 11:00 p.m., arriving at Aunt Helen's at midnight. My eighty-four-year-old aunt was standing at the stove in her housedress, smiling, laughing, talking, and keeping warm the five-course meal she had spent the entire day preparing. We sat, telling stories and enjoying the delicious feast. Aunt Helen encouraged us to get to bed while she packed up the meal so we could enjoy it with Dad the next day. Pat and I said good night and went up to her bedroom on the second floor, an uncharted land. The kitchen looked new but hardly modern with red and white cabinets and "retro" appliances, silverware, and dishes, a room out of a forties' *Life Magazine*. The living room, dinning room, and bedroom were of museum quality; 1940 stood still in Aunt Helen's house. But more than the furnishings, I remember her flexibility on our late-night visit from Seattle and appreciate it even more today.

I visited Dad three or four times a year and, on most visits, also saw Helen. On one trip, Dad and I had dinner at Porto Bello. Walking home through the neighborhood, we encountered rain, and Dad looked wistfully at pea caps in a store window. He reminisced, "In the thirties, I had a pea cap like that. I looked good in a pea cap. Those were the good old days."

I entered the store and purchased two pea caps. "Here put this on; let's see if you look good in it."

He placed it on his head, looking at his reflection between the raindrops in the store window. "I still look pretty good." Laughing with our new pea caps on, we continued walking home in the rain.

The next day we visited Aunt Helen. As we got out of the cab with our pea caps, Helen put her hands to the side of her face while shrieking and laughing, saying, "I wish Vera could see you two today. What a sight, a heck of a pair to draw to."

We spent the day, and as evening approached, preparing to leave, Dad excused himself to go to the bathroom, leaving Helen and me alone in the kitchen. Helen leaned across the table and held my hands, saying, "You and your family should move back. We would all so love it, and it would be good for your father."

I looked across the table at Helen's wet eyes and held her trembling hands. "We all need to live our own lives, be happy, and do the right thing. I know how hard this is on Dad and you. I love you both very much and would never do anything to hurt you. I love you as I love my mom."

Helen stood up, wiped her eyes, and tightly hugging me, said, "I know, but life is hard and sometimes lonely."

My aunt lived two years after our pea-cap appearance at her house. Although visiting several more times, we never had time alone again for me to express how much I appreciated all she had done for me. But as I typed these words, I am sure Aunt Helen looked over my shoulder, smiling and proud of all she had accomplished.

Mom, Aunt Helen and Aunt Mamie

Uncle Albert

Uncle Albert and Aunt Antoinetta had three children, Rita, Benny, and Gloria. Uncle Albert worked in New York City, commuting by ferry and subway two hours a day from Staten Island. Albert was Mom's oldest brother, the patriarch of the family after Nonno died. But even before then, as the oldest male child, he held with his father the responsibility for the family when in Italy and in this country, working with his father and supporting his extended family. No wonder that Uncle Albert, a manual laborer, always worked two or more jobs at a time.

My nonno gave a great gift to his oldest son, the love of gardening. Uncle Albert and Aunt Antoinetta spent many a day in their garden, which produced a bounty year after year.

Mom, Dad, and I visited my uncle many times in Staten Island. After the long trip, before taking coats off, we went to see the garden. I tagged along, listening, knowing I was on sacred ground. Respecting and somewhat fearing my uncle, I recognized he would not tolerate a child running wild in his garden.

When I was in New York visiting Mom and Dad before going to Vietnam; we visited Uncle Albert and Aunt Antoinetta. Uncle Albert and I found ourselves alone outside, walking through the garden. He proudly pointed to tomato plants he had started from seed, now full of tomatoes, which shortly would be ready for the table. Reaching over I held a large tomato still attached to its branch, admiring it. Albert took my hand, pulling it and the tomato within it to him. He took the tomato from my hand and, with his pocketknife, cut the tomato in quarters, presenting them to me. I took a quarter, put it in my mouth, shut my eyes, and said, "*Buono. Grazie.*" My uncle gave me a full-moon smile, his wet eyes twinkling. His right arm was on my shoulder; pulling my head down, he kissed my cheek. Arms intertwined, we walked into the house.

It was not until forty years later when his son, Benny, died that I recognized the significance of that visit. Benny and I became one to my uncle. The time was not 1968; it was 1943. Benny and I were leaving for a war; we might not return. His memories of saying goodbye to his son found their way into our visit.

Cousin Benny was my godfather. Although twenty-five years apart, we were close friends, knowing each other better than the rest of the family knew us, bonded by our time in the service. We spent time together, laughing, telling funny family stories, understanding each other. Although never having intimate conversations, we knew each other so well we didn't need them. Benny was a loving and gentle man, possessing humility, a great sense of humor, and respect for everyone.

On one trip to New York after Dads' death, Pat and I had dinner with Benny and my other three remaining cousins. During the evening, he and I excused ourselves from the dining table, entered the living room, and had our first private conversation.

Benny had a reputation for spending less than thirty minutes when visiting family members, even with the Head Aunt. I asked him jokingly why.

He laughed. "You want to know why? I'll tell you, but you need to know I never told anyone until now. It's the first time I was asked. Every time I visit someone, we spend the first ten or twenty minutes getting caught up. After that, they start to complain and I wind up hearing things that I don't want to hear about, which make me sad, so I leave. You should try it; it works." He held my hand; I held my side, laughing until we cried.

Joe and Helen with
Nonna, Antoinetta,
and Albert

Benny with daughter
Diane; Rita and Gloria
standing, Nonna sitting

Benny, World War II

Drafted into the Army in World War II, Benny spent time overseas. We never spoke about his tour of duty or discussed my time in the Army. Our relationship had no need for such conversation. The year of our visit coincided with the fiftieth anniversary of Victory in Europe. Benny was the oldest active World War II member of his American Legion Post and requested to speak during the anniversary observation. Benny declined. I asked him why.

He responded, "That was a long time ago, and I don't have much to say." He then told me a little about his time in the service with many sideway glances in my direction, telling me by his eyes. Benny asked if I wrote any stories about my time in the Army.

"I wrote only one."

"I'd like to read it."

"I will mail you a copy as soon as I get back to Seattle."

Benny, diagnosed with lung cancer and knowing the finality of his prognosis, elected to decline additional treatment, living the time he had as best he could. Benny and his wife, Sarah, went home early that same evening. A few hours before, he had been discharged from the hospital, and both felt exhausted from the strain of the past several days. Benny insisted Pat and I visit him before leaving the next day for Seattle.

We arrived at Benny and Sarah's house and had lunch, laughing and talking about the family. Benny stood with difficulty and took out of his desk a manila envelope. Extending the envelope to me, he said, "This is a letter I sent to the family from England during the war. I want you to read it." The letter had arrived home after he had transferred from England into France. I read it aloud to Sarah, Benny's wife, his sisters, and Pat.

Tears filled every eye in the kitchen as we heard the words written decades before by this proud, gentle man to his beloved ones at home.

Benny died three weeks later. The story I sent him he never had an opportunity to read.

War has the ability to cut to the quick. Without much time, you think, "What really is important?" a question worthy of being asked every day.

Cousin Jamesie

Named after his father, Jamesie was the oldest of the Rosso children. I first met my cousin when he returned from the Philippines after World War II. I was standing in my crib in Mom and Dad's bedroom when Jamesie arrived in his Army uniform, smiled, and walked over to the crib, picking me up for the first time. We saw each other almost every day thereafter, but I remember most his presence in my adolescence.

Jamesie took me to the Paramount Theater. We waited in line on a sweltering, breezeless New York summer day when temperature and humidity were one, three hours for tickets to see Frank Sinatra. This was my first live stage show. What an introduction to live performances!

We stood in line together again at seven in the morning several years later during the last week of December with the temperature below zero and a nor'easter howling in our ears for over two hours to get seats for the NFL Championship between the Giants and the Colts, Charlie Conerly quarterback for the Giants versus Johnny Unitas for the Colts. We watched the first half, bodies shaking, teeth chattering, sipping on lukewarm coffee.

As the second half began, I left for the nearest bathroom. Opening the door, I felt a rush of warm air as smoke assaulted my nose and eyes. The room was aglow, paper towels, newspaper, and wooden seat backs, were on fire in a metal wastebasket. I missed most of the third quarter, warming my frigid body in the restroom fire. Returning to my seat, Jamesie asked, "What took you so long?" I never replied as a fumble occurred and everyone stood, the roar drowning out any conversation. Trying to forget the cold, I focused on the time clock, watching every second tick off, anxious to leave to a heated place to stop the shaking. Time ran out on the scoreboard clock but resulted in no mass exodus from the stadium and the cold. Shocked, I looked back at the scoreboard. The game was tied 21 to 21! After five minutes passed, the sun set, plunging the temperature even further. The public address system announcer said, "We will now be playing sudden death," a most appropriate term. The teams would continue to play until one team scored—or all the fans died of frostbite. The Colts won. I think. We left the stadium. It was now after five o'clock. Darkness set in, accompanied by a biting winter wind. I remember Jamesie giving me his scarf, taking me to the nearest luncheonette to make the shivering stop. Presented with the menu, he smiled and asked me, "Do you want some ice cream, a nice cold soda?"

One place Jamesie took me to without a waiting line was Aqueduct Racetrack. Jamesie, like everyone in the neighborhood, was a handicapper, one who studied the race forms, past performances, existing track conditions, jockey, weight carried, length of the race, and every other piece of information available to determine which horse in an eight- to ten-horse field had the best chance to win. Contrary to his calculations and findings, a neighborhood myth took precedence in his decisions: "Gray horses are always long shots, but potential miracles. Always bet a gray horse. Miracles happen. But not to us." After several trips to the track and handicapping tutoring, I concluded, based on experience, we did not have a snowball's chance in hell of winning. I enjoyed the weather, the race, the excitement of being there, and the illegal beer. The temperature was warm; the line to the two-dollar window was short. What more could you ask for?

Jamesie had spent some of his Army time in the mess hall and extended this training to his home, becoming the Rosso family gourmet chef, much to his father and mother's dismay. Entering Apartment #54 late one afternoon, Aunt Rosie was in the kitchen, her hands on the back of a chair, staring at her son at the stove. A cast-iron kettle was on the stovetop with other smaller pots and pans, flames and smoke billowing from the uncovered kettle.

"What's he cooking, Aunt Rosie?"

"Don't ask me; ask your cousin."

The chef turned his head through the smoke and answered, "I'm cooking French. The dish is called roast duck à l'orange."

I had no idea what he was talking about.

Jamesie asked, "Do you want to know about the l'orange sauce and how it's prepared?"

"No. I can't believe anyone in his right mind would cook and eat a goddamn duck."

The dish, like several following, was always different, interesting, and suitable for one to two polite tastes.

Jamesie worked part-time for his dad at the funeral parlor as a chauffeur while working full time as a bartender at Husk's bar on Spring and Thompson Streets. One job many times immediately followed the other, forcing Jamesie to take every opportunity to prepare for his next shift. On slow afternoons, he typically found a quiet place to catch a few winks when no one was around.

Aunt Rose was shopping for a holiday family dinner, and Mom had enlisted my aid as a bag Sherpa. We left Faiocco's pork store, the vegetable and fruit pushcarts, and Rocco's pastry shop on Bleecker Street. Heading back to Sullivan Street, Aunt Rosie said, "Let's stop at the funeral parlor before we head to Phil and Pete the butcher and see if Jamesie needs any help."

We entered the funeral parlor. Empty, with Jamesie nowhere around. We called. No answer. Finally we found Jamesie in the casket storage area in the basement, sound asleep in an open casket. Aunt Rosie marched over to the open coffin, shaking his arm, and demanded, "What the hell are you doing sleeping? What if someone came down here and shut the lid on the casket? What would you do then?"

Jamesie opened his eyes, looking around to get his bearings, turned to his mother with a smile, and replied, "I guess I wouldn't be driving the hearse tomorrow."

One of the many rites of passage in our neighborhood was obtaining a driver's license. Everybody knew the date of your eighteenth birthday, which made you eligible to sign up for your driving test. If you failed to take your driver's license test within a month of your birthday, there was something seriously wrong with you. Rumors passed through the neighborhood, as they did on any day, but today the topic was you. Smiles, glances, and shakes of the head previously welcomed now seemed more like threats. Getting a driver's license was passage to manhood. But Dad did not own a car and did not have a driver's license, both of which were two of the many prerequisites to taking the test. A second month passed since the magic birthday. Still searching for a solution to the problem, I spoke to Jamesie, and we developed a plan to acquire a car with a licensed driver being present to take the test. I would schedule the license exam for a day Jamesie was off work, provide the cash for him to rent a car, and he would accompany me to take the driving test.

The morning of the test, we rented an ugly, green, four-door, Ford Fairlane. The driving test was not until two that afternoon, so we had some time with my permit and Jamesie's presence for me to practice for my driving test.

We agreed I would drive the car through the neighborhood. Jamesie would act as the examiner, and I would explicitly follow all his directions. Everything was going well. I executed hand signals as well as directional signals, parallel parked, and made right and left turns. On Houston Street a busy four-lane street, Jamesie told me to get into the left-hand lane. I did as the light turned red. I stopped. The light changed to green. While I remained in my spot, a chorus of horns and curses erupted behind us.

Jamesie turned, yelling above the din, "Why the hell don't you make a left turn?"

"You never told me to make a left turn."

"Well make one now, goddamn it."

Several minutes passed as we headed up West Broadway. Meanwhile, Jamesie's neck veins deflated, and his face returned to white. "When you are driving, you have to pay attention at all times to the road. Anticipation and concentration are everything. You have to be focused. Lives depend on your judgment. You can't watch a pretty blonde in a red coat; black short skirt, and high heels get into a car."

Jamesie married Ann who was college educated and not from the neighborhood. On her first visit to our apartment, she presented my parents and me with gifts. A freshman in high school, I excitedly opened my gift. "What the hell is this?" It was a book. We had four books in our entire apartment in addition to my textbooks—a prayer book, a first-aid manual, my dad's radio and television repair book, and another one I do not remember. No one in the neighborhood ever gave books as presents. I gave her a hug, sat on the couch while everyone was in the kitchen, and paged through a book by James Thurber. I read the book not because I had to but because I wanted to.

Several years later, Ann became ill, her doctor recommending that she and Jamesie relocate to be near her family in Buffalo. Jamesie, with no financial resources, left the neighborhood, family, and support group, living thirty-five years in Buffalo. Ann did not improve, eventually requiring full-time institutional care. Jamesie visited her every day for the rest of his life, one that ended too soon. He died before I completed this book. The last time I saw my cousin was the afternoon I visited his mother in the hospital over twenty-five years ago. I wish I had told him how much he meant to me.

Cousins Gloria and Rita

The daughters of Uncle Albert and Aunt Antoinette, the younger sisters of Benny, are inseparable, living close to each other, sharing laughter, hardships, and pains of aging. As the eighth decade of their life approaches, their relationship remains as close as it was in their early teens.

My cousins learned from their father the primacy of family, the importance of respect for all, and the art of giving. Uncle Albert unselfishly gave of himself, always finding time or making time to provide support to family members. He took seriously his position as the oldest and gave the most, asking nothing in return. Rita and Gloria learned from his example and took care of their dad with his cancer into his seventies. After my uncle died, they continued to take care of their mother, Antoinetta, housebound over fifteen years, until her ninetieth year. In addition to taking care of their mom, they teamed with their cousin Gilda, who was their age and living close by, to continue their father's art of giving, first under the direction of Helen the Head Aunt while she was alive, then on their own.

Gloria, Rita, and Gilda visited family members in the hospital and at home, bringing prepared and purchased food, pastries, fruit, and sometimes even sneaking in the much appreciated red wine and grappa. Family members, sick or living alone, became their priority, receiving foods, shopping services, household chores, and chauffeuring to doctors, hospitals, and drug stores. The three cousins visited my mom after her hospitalization and mastectomy two to three times a month. On every occasion, they washed the floors, changed the linens on the bed, and went shopping five floors below to Sullivan Street, then participated in cooking a meal that always had several days of leftovers. The visits to Sullivan Street continued until my dad moved to Seattle. Most trips took a day of their time, a day away from their immediate family and their own needs. Telephone calls among the extended family occurred every week or two, keeping everyone informed of relatives and friends and their needs. All family members knew throughout their life that they belonged to a family that cared and loved them and they would never be alone. Birthday cards, anniversary cards, Mass cards, and care packages filled in the time between phone calls. As the years passed, it was Gloria and Rita who visited Gilda weekly in her assisted living facility, continuing the lifelong support.

Upon Aunt Helen's death, Gloria became the "Head Cousin." We had no primary election, no vote, no Electoral College, just Gloria's inherent desire to keep the magic of family alive. As her predecessor did, Gloria as the Head Cousin arranges for those with needs to have them met, keeping alive the bonds of family through giving and receiving, with support and comfort. Over the years, as the number of family members has declined significantly, Gloria has become the doer as well as the planner. She monitors all the family; and we continue to stay in touch through telephone calls, cards, and packages on the holidays. We, in turn, keep the connection strong with visits to our cousins in New York. Gloria delivers both happy and sad messages to family, keeps everyone aware of each other, and through her work reminds us that we are still a family. No one of us travels through this world alone because of her efforts and her love.

We keep alive the values our grandparents and great-grandparents instilled in us by passing them on to the next generation with our example. Our family continues the tradition of visiting the cemeteries honoring the dead. We maintain gravesites, placing wreaths and planting flowers on holy days, saying prayers, telling stories of the deceased. We pray for their souls, promising they will not be forgotten.

My cousins preformed this role for the entire family, visiting gravesites in Staten Island and Queens, a task that took more than a single day thirty years ago and much longer today. Pat and I, on a recent trip to New York, visited all the family gravesites with Cousin Gloria. We reminisced about each family member, laughing, crying, and silently standing at the gravesite with our individual thoughts. We relived our lives through the dates on the gravestones, each a milestone along our lifelong journey as well. Graves of close friends and neighbors, thanks to Uncle Jimmy, surround those of our family members, reminding us of our greater connection to the whole community. Their faces, too, all but disappeared from our consciousness, now recalled, causing smiles and tears with the expanded memories. The cemetery, silent, subdued, sacred, filled us once more with stories of family, old friends, and laughter.

Accordion Cousins

Aunt Katie and Uncle Willie had one daughter, Gilda. Gilda married James Donnelly, living on Staten Island. Over the years, Jimmy and Gilda with Aunt Helen's guidance transported relatives to family gatherings, helped to schedule functions, and worked with the Head Aunt to ensure the family was together and cared for.

Gilda and Jimmy's son, Jimmy Jr., was my age, but we saw each other only at family functions since Staten Island for my folks involved a half-day trip using public transportation. Benny and Sara with their two children, Diane, the oldest, and Robert, lived in Staten Island less than a half mile from Jimmy and Gilda. Benny's family assisted Gilda and Jimmy in carrying out the Head Aunt's directions for family functions, and their son, Robert, was strongly influenced by his older cousin Jimmy.

At each family gathering, Cousin Jimmy was encouraged to play his accordion, which he did with great ability. Without warning, Cousin Robert took up the accordion, and now both loudly played to the applause of family and friends. Where had I gone wrong? I felt a traitor to my heritage as I pretended to appreciate these reputed virtuosos, politely applauding and, with a forced smile, silently asking God to rescue me as quickly as possible from my earthly purgatory. I admit I had no natural or acquired musical ability; I could barely turn on the radio. I listened to rock and roll, to Sinatra and Bennett, never hearing an accordion as accompaniment. Somehow had I missed the lesson in accordion appreciation. Instead, if requested to add to Dante's description of the underworld, I would include, "Spending eternity listening to 'Lady of Spain' played on the accordion."

Robert's older sister, Diane, with a smile and infectious laugh brought joy to everyone around her. Diane married Bobbie in her mid thirties and moved to Florida. Three years after leaving Staten Island, she was diagnosed with leukemia and given less than a year to live. Robert, working in the Fulton Fish Market, spoke to his boss and, laptop in hand, flew to Florida to be with his sister during her last months. Like Aunt Helen caring for her sister Mamie, Robert provided that shoulder for Diane to rest on, to cry on.

The week before Christmas many years ago, Cousin Jimmy and his wife rented a stretch limo. The posh transport picked up Jimmy's mom and dad, Gilda and Jimmy, then Aunt Helen, and finally, driving to Sullivan Street, Mom and Dad. With Christmas music in the background, the limo took its occupants up Sixth Avenue, past Macy's and Gimbels, past Broadway, to Central Park, through the park, past the Plaza Hotel, Tiffany's, Rockefeller Center, Saint Patrick's Cathedral, spending time at each. What a fabulous gift.

To the accordion players, "Bless them all."

Cousin Rosemary

Rosemary Rosso is Jamesie's younger sister, my surrogate sister, and six years my senior. We grew up together with one flight of stairs separating us. Listening from our kitchen windows, we could hear the loud conversations of our parents providing strong guidance. We would run to the rescue, showing up unannounced at the other's apartment, a timely interruption, the adults none the wiser for our ploy. We spent time in the apartments together after school and dinner, watching TV, playing gin rummy, or just telling stories of the neighborhood and the day's gossip. Out in the neighborhood, a different code of behavior prevailed. We each had our own group of friends where guys stuck with guys and girls with girls. But as we got older, we did spend time together in public, especially going to the movies at Waverly Place, and Rosemary became my escort out of the apartment. Thanks to her chaperoning, I got to see some great movies, *From Here to Eternity* and *On the Waterfront*, while practicing the art of tossing Juicy Fruits at unsuspecting moviegoers. Playing her part well, my cousin merely giggled quietly in the background

During the holidays, parents relegated kids to the kitchen due to limited space at the big table in the living room. Making the best of the situation, Rosemary practiced her culinary skills on the big-table exiles. Whatever remained on the table, on the stove, in the refrigerator, and

Rosemary and the author on the roof of 120 Sullivan

within reach got mixed, sliced, chopped, stirred, and then served to the unfortunates. She served the concoctions cold or hot but mostly al dente. Words fail to describe the unsavoriness that reached our mouths or the pain that settled in our stomachs. Saving us from further damage, by the time we exiles lost our willingness to eat her creations, Rosemary, as a teenager, lost her desire to become a chef.

At around the same time that she passed her culinary stage, a young couple from the neighborhood moved into the middle apartment on the fifth floor, Apartment #63. Arthur and Jeanette, in their late twenties and an immediate hit with all the tenants, asked Rosemary to baby-sit for their first child, Barbara. Although nervous at first, Rosemary relaxed under the couple's easing her into the responsibility. Aware of my cousin's concerns, Arthur and Jeanette, intelligent, playful, and with a great sense of humor, gave her several short trial runs. Feeling confident with those successes, Rosemary graduated to services regularly requested on Friday or Saturday nights. Saturday night was not a problem but Friday night was.

On Friday nights, a buck up front guaranteed my presence to assist my cousin, not for baby-sitting but to "assist" Rosemary in watching the two-hour horror movie showcased on TV. She loved those movies, but she felt comfortable viewing them in the apartment only with someone present who could yell for help when the werewolf attacked. That was my job.

Never being close to a baby so tiny, so helpless, I went through my apprenticeship with my cousin and received excellent training for raising my children, feeding, changing, cleaning, and most important, holding and loving them.

The horror show previewed the next week's movie at the end of the program. When I learned that next week's movie would show the most popular—for not only Rosemary but the entire neighborhood—*Dracula*, I spent most of my free time that next week with glue, paper, scissors, balsa wood, string, and paint, constructing a three-foot-wide black bat kite with red eyes, attached to a line on a fishing pole. On Friday night, I waited well into one of the scariest parts of *Dracula*, during the commercial, saying, "Rosemary, I need to get something from the apartment. I'll be right back." Closing the door, I ran to the roof where I had hidden the bat kite and fishing pole. Standing above the open window, bat kite and fishing pole in hand, I waited for the voice of Dracula. Hearing his master's voice, I lowered the kite until it was adjacent to the upper glass window. Moving the fishing pole rapidly and banging the bat into the glass window, I scored: Rosemary's scream drowned out Dracula's voice. Laughing, I ran down to rescue my cousin. Rosemary, looking through fingers in front of her eyes and seeing the bat kite in my hand, clenched her fingers into a fist and rose from the couch just as Barbara awoke, crying and saving my life.

I flew the bat kite one other Friday night. The victim was my mom. My screams drowned out the vampires.

Rosemary oriented Pat and our children to the family, its traditions, and taboos and spoiled our children when we visited. My cousin took our children to her apartment or down onto Sullivan Street, providing us precious time to visit quietly in the cramped apartment. We walked the neighborhood, Rosemary telling stories of the people and places we passed. Guidance was provided on where to eat, what to order, and where to go. She knew us and provided us an education on the neighborhood, changed since our last visit. Before we confirmed our family visit to New York, we spoke to Rosemary. "Is this a good time to come? What's going on in the family? Is everyone well? What's new in the neighborhood?"

Rosemary arranged for Mom and Dad's thirty-fifth anniversary surprise party at a restaurant in the neighborhood, and Aunt Helen managed to get the entire family to be present. Our Seattle family flew in midweek, and on Saturday, we left Apartment #64 for a presumed quiet family dinner. With the whole family present, there is no such thing as quiet. Mom and Dad were proud and happy, their smiles covering every square inch of the room. Our children tell stories of collecting money from family members to play songs on the jukebox, never played. Four-year-old Annemarie in a frilly white dress sat at the bar with a Shirley Temple next to her benefactor, a lieutenant in the local Mafia. Rosemary introduced him to the entire family; he graciously shook hands with Dad and gave Mom a kiss, providing bottles of red wine for the family's enjoyment.

After Mom's death, Rosemary became Dad's daughter, alerting me of his needs, providing me the reason to travel to New York for support without Dad ever having to ask. Telephone calls occurred daily, visits weekly, and holidays and birthdays never forgotten. She bridged the loss of my mom for me by being there for Dad.

After Dad died, our visits always included Rosemary, the family historian, keeping us mesmerized and laughing at her kitchen table much as her mother did in Apartment #54, with similar dark twinkling eyes. Sitting with her and hearing the stories transported me back again to the fifties; nothing had changed. I could see Sullivan Street , the café on the corner of Prince Street with black Cadillacs and the wise guys in white dress shirts, Dick the tailor sweeping the sidewalk in front of his shop, Jack and Alice and their dog, "Thor," Mr. De Bol, Fat Joe, the detectives in their unmarked car, faces and voices from our childhood.

Dad and Rosemary

Mom

Writing about my parents in the past tense is difficult for they still share every day with me. I finally realize and understand the love they provided. Love flowed to our family with every conversation, letter, telephone call, and visit. We were the center of my parent's universe, an extension of their dreams.

Today's American Dream is one of conspicuous consumption, having two houses, two cars, two jobs, and two good incomes. My parents had no house, no car, no checking account or credit cards, no investments, no new furniture, and no vacations. Dad had a steady job, his salary modest by the standard of the time, supporting a wife, son, and his parents, and helping other family members and friends when needed. My parents never bought into the American Dream; they had their Italian Dream, a happy marriage fulfilled with the gifts of family, friends, children, and grandchildren. Our family frowned upon discussing your good fortune or showing off possessions that others did not have, expressing concern a person who was not doing well might be hurt upon seeing or hearing about your good fortune. My parents based their values solely on people not things. Mom's mantra was, "Life is hard enough; don't make it any harder. Respect those around you. If you wish for anything, wish for health and happiness; the rest is bullshit."

Mom and Dad's Wedding

Mom—Elvira Ann DeVincenzi, Vera, the second youngest of six children, born in 1915—was the center of my life and always there for me. I trusted her, knowing she would protect me from harm and unpleasantness, sacrificing her needs for my well-being. I knew no matter what I did, how horrible, shameful, and disgraceful, I could knock on the door of Apartment #64 at any hour, and at the unlocked door Mom would shower me with hugs and love. I know now what that means, unconditional love. I grew up blessed.

Ingrained in every family member was a work ethic. Mom was no exception, working as a child and learning from her parents, older brother, Albert, and sister, Helen. Mom graduated DeVincenzis with a master's degree in hard work. On holidays, she was responsible for preparing the special dinner for guests and family. Holiday meals required Mom to spend hours of planning followed by more hours of preparation and cooking and baking. Her presence and warmth more than the meal made the day special. Mom knew how to work and, more important, how to play. She had a mischievous, playful, happy loving child constantly springing out of her adult body. Mom asked for little, cheerfully giving of herself to make others happy, no strings attached. She gave unconditional love to family and to friends.

Mom was religious but not fanatical, having a special relationship with her God. Her God was there when someone died, when someone was sick, when the money ran out. Her God was there when Mom bet on a horse, bet on a number, or sat down to play a game of poker.

Mom's happiest times were playing the role of grandmother, spending every moment she could with her grandchildren, making them happy. She taught them to laugh and to dream, making their wishes come true and, in turn, making her wishes reality. Mom said, "Our lives are about the babies, God's "wonderful gifts."

Mom's life, as everyone's on Sullivan Street, was not easy with an eighth-grade education, working with her parents and sisters during her grade-school years, maintaining 120 Sullivan Street. Shortly after graduating from grade school, the Depression of 1929 occurred. Mom now worked with her sisters in the garment factories, sweatshops bordering the neighborhood. After a ten-hour day sewing in the factory, she helped her parents, stoking the furnace, loading and cleaning garbage cans. After eating a late dinner, she sat down with her sisters at the kitchen table, making artificial flowers, paid by the piece for each flower completed, some requiring as many as five to fifteen different tasks.

Doctors diagnosed her younger sister Mamie with a very aggressive cancer, requiring several disfiguring operations to her face. My loving aunt had her nose removed to avert the spread of the beast to the rest of what was left of her face. Her wound required cleaning and bandage changes several times a day. Mom quit her sweatshop job to help care for her younger sister while continuing to work with her mom and dad maintaining 120 Sullivan Street. Money was difficult to come by. Without health insurance, the costs of Mamie's cancer required everyone's support; working more than one job was a necessity. The family pooled their resources to pay for Mamie's cancer treatment; the dollar cost was significant, but the emotional cost of losing your younger sister was devastating. Laughter and tears became one. Mom continued helping family and friends for her entire life.

We had only one appliance in our apartment—a gas stove. The apartments had no dishwashing machine, clothes washer, or dryer. Iceboxes kept food cold; only later did refrigerators replace them. Buying and preparing food, washing and mending clothes for a family of five, staying within budget took planning and hard work. After assisting her parents and taking care of her sister, Mom shopped for food every day. She walked five to seven blocks, buying bread at the bakery, cheese at the cheese store, vegetables at the vegetable store or pushcarts, and *sopressata* at the pork store, stopping at the butcher shop and finally the grocery store, to place her bet on today's number and purchase anything else she needed. She carried shopping bags up five flights of stairs, unpacking, and preparing dinner. To stretch the dollar, she selected the least expensive meats and chicken, which required long cooking times to tenderize. She set the table, served the meal, washed and dried the dishes, put them away, took the dog up to the roof, took out the garbage. Not yet done for the day, Mom continued her work washing clothes in the kitchen sink, accompanied by the sound of the

Big Bands playing on the radio. Planning began for tomorrow and coffee prepared for the morning. She had few breaks in the routine.

Dad, six years older, married Mom on his thirty-first birthday. Her family that day increased to four, Dad's parents moving with him into Apartment #64. Papa John had lost his job as a barber after suffering from a stroke that affected his right hand. Mom's role expanded, but so did her smile. Within three years, I was born, adding more work to Mom's load—and, I suspect, widening her smile.

Mom said, "The day you were born, I never saw your father after we arrived at the hospital. Aunt Helen came, staying with me through labor and delivery. Your dad spent the night restricted to the waiting room. We finally saw him after you were born. He entered the room with a smile, holding my hand, reaching over to hold yours, never saying a word. After a long silence, I said, 'Tony! Are you all right? Do you need a chair?' Still holding both our hands, looking at me, smiling, he said, 'All is well, thank God,' making the sign of the cross on his forehead."

One humid summer morning, Mom left me at Aunt Rosie's apartment while she went shopping. The phone rang. Rosie picked up the receiver. I could tell by my aunt's voice something was wrong. She hung up, shaking her head. Seeing my stare, a smile appeared together with a biscotti. Mom returned laden with shopping bags and sweat and put the shopping bags on the kitchen floor. While Mom was lifting the bags to the table and separating the contents, Rosie told her about the telephone call. A cousin twenty years younger had lost her husband unexpectedly to a heart attack. Mom stopped unpacking, shook her head in disbelief, and sobbed. The last bag was still on the floor, the sweat still on her forehead. "Watch Anthony. I'm going to Saint Anthony's to say a rosary and light a candle. I'll light one for you." Mom believed the number of prayers said for the deceased and the number of candles lit in their behalf could influence God's judgment on where their souls would spend eternity.

Mom was a physically strong woman, never asking for assistance moving furniture or carrying packages. Many women in our building asked Mom for assistance. Mom washed windows in the tenement for additional money. The weathered wood window frames over time became loose in their casings, moving sideways when touched. Cracked putty held the windowpane in the casing, the windowpane rattling in the casing when the window closed or opened. Dressed in a cotton housedress, Mom sat on the windowsill, her torso outside, legs dangling inside the apartment, careful to avoid the hot radiator. Her shoes were "neighborhood issue," sling-back wedgies, open toed, low heeled, black in color. She wore cut-off, rolled-down nylons, a holdover from World War II. During the war, nylons were difficult to obtain. Once the nylons got a run, women cut the nylon off at or above the run, making ankle-or knee-high stockings.

Mom's upper body extended above Sullivan Street, hanging onto the bottom of the window's wooden frame, leaning out to wash the window, first the top, then the bottom. Nonna, four foot nine inches, one hundred pounds or less, held Mom's legs. This act of safety never provided solace to me. I could see my nonna hurtling to her death, holding onto her daughter's legs. Washing windows in our building always frightened me. I shut my eyes, attempting to avoid my imagination. Today looking from Sullivan Street to the fifth floor, I shake my head in disbelief.

Big Mamma grew up on Thompson Street and was an early advocate for women's rights at a time when most women in the neighborhood treated Italian men as royalty, as the authority in the family, and with great respect. Big Mamma, Aunt Rosie, and Mom did attend to their duties as proper Italian wives and homemakers. But the trio also used their sense of humor to put these lords and kings in their place with sarcastic remarks and observations, bringing laughter to those in attendance. Nothing was sacred.

Big Mamma mentored her daughter-in-law in playing gin and five-and seven-card stud poker. My grandmother taught Mom how to bet numbers straight or in combination, with introductory advice on betting horses. Bets were placed through neighborhood bookies at the storefront café in the building, grocery stores, bars, and candy stores. The café in our building provided a place to store groceries, sip coffee, place bets, and visit with friends while watching the kids play in the street, prior to carrying the bags up the stairs to their apartments. Big

The Vivolo's at Helen and Joe's house

Mamma, Aunt Rosie, and Mom became kindred spirits. After shopping and cleaning the apartment with the dinner meal brought to a slow boil then lowered to simmer, Big Mamma began to shuffle the cards. It was time for another lesson and laughter.

When no adult was available, I played cards with Mom and Big Mamma, as a third player made the game more interesting and added a greater element of chance. To provide focus, Mom placed a piece of cheese, a cookie, or candy on the table as an incentive for me to pay attention and try to win the hand. Mom loved to play gin, after Big Mamma's death I became her stand-in. We played two out of three, or four out of seven games for food or drink incentives. If we played for a salami sandwich, it was two out of three with the loser making sandwiches. If we played for Entenmann's coffee cake, which required a trip to the grocery store, it was four out of seven. We spent many hours playing gin, sharing thoughts, fears, and wishes, much as she did with her mother-in-law.

During first grade, Mom walked me to Saint Anthony's School at 60 MacDougal Street. Our walk took us by a neighborhood bakery, and sometimes she bought a cookie or jelly doughnut for my brown paper lunch bag.

During one of Pat and my visits to the neighborhood, we noticed Saint Anthony's School was open although school was not in session. We entered and, with permission, walked through the mostly unchanged halls. As we left the school, Pat noticed the words "Boys" and "Girls" carved into the arches over the two brown entry doors. Spending eight years at the school, I had never noticed the carved words, or if I did, I had paid no attention to them. The boys always entered the north door, guarded by a rotund nun, watching for contraband bubble gum, slices of pizza, jelly doughnuts, baseballs, comic books, or anything declared disruptive to receiving a quality education. The girls entered through the nun-less south door.

Separation of girls and boys also occurred outside of grade school. The girls walked together to or from grade school, no boys allowed.

Parents or relatives escorted girls to and from Saint Anthony's for eight years. Sullivan Street was always full of unsupervised boys playing every sport imaginable; girls were nowhere in sight. Supervision began to break down in the last year of grade school, and we boys discovered these lovely creatures, living—much to our surprise—on Sullivan Street.

On First Friday of each month, the entire school attended mass. All who had made their First Communion, usually those in grades two and above, were expected to receive that sacrament at mass. But first we had to be in a pure and holy state, which meant confessing our sins to a priest. So on Thursdays before First Fridays, the sisters of Saint Anthony's grade school took us from school by class to the church to receive the sacrament of confession. They divided the eighth grade class into two groups in our classroom, the girls with headscarves led by Sister Theresa Marie, the boys led by Mother Bonita, Sister Stephen, and Sister John Joseph.

We entered the main aisle at the back of the church. The girls, upon the click of Sister Theresa Marie's metal ladybug, genuflected in unison, making the sign of the cross. On the next click, the girls stood in unison, with hands folded in prayer, entering, six to a pew, the last three rows on the right side of the center aisle. The boys needed more help. Mother Bonita's clap of her stubby thick hands signaled our start, and with Sister Stephen's outstretched arms directing each boy and Sister John Joseph's selective ear pulls, we entered the four rear pews on the left side of the church, six more or less in each. Two priests, carrying prayer books and wearing cassocks over which were draped confession shawls, left the altar, headed to the rear of the church, and entered confessionals to the right and left of the center aisle. As usual, the girls got the easier priest to hear their confessions.

Mother Bonita, still standing in the center aisle, signaled the class to kneel, directing the boys and girls of Saint Anthony's to recite together an Act of Contrition and prepare to confess their sins.

Sister Theresa Marie stood behind her girls, bowed her head, and began saying the rosary on her prayer beads. Her charges, hearing the prayers, responded accordingly. On the boys' side, Mother Bonita stood in the center aisle, brown eyes glaring at pew inhabitants giving sneaky open-handed dope slaps to the back heads of silent, obedient, front-pew inhabitants. Sister John Joseph, the same height as her charges, occupied the pew directly in front of the noisy boys but never sat or knelt. She paced back and forth, finger or hand thrust into the chest of the head-bobbling, gum-chewing, giggling, and elbowing disrupters. Sister Stephen, older and taller than her counterparts, conducted inspection from the rear, recording in her ever-present black book the names of irreverent individuals for after-school detention.

The girls, one by one, signaled by Sister Theresa Marie's ladybug clicker, entered the unoccupied portion of the confessional. Within seconds, the small sliding screen that the priest had opened in the private confessional to hear the girl's sins closed. The penitent quickly exited the confessional, walked with head down to the altar at the front of the church, and began reciting the prayers the priest had assigned as penance. On the other side of the center aisle, a different scene unfolded.

Sister John Joseph stood before the two boys closest to the center aisle, a location none of the guys wanted to be caught dead in, the first row. Using her frog clicker, hand, and finger as encouragement, she directed the first pew penitents. Hands clasped together and heads bowed, though lacking the reverence of the girls, they began their trek to the confessional.

The rest of us, not being first to go to confession, let our attentions drift. The church's solemn silence suddenly shattered.

"No way is Mantle better than Mays."

"Stop farting, Ritchie. God you stink."

"Who hit me?"

"Vinnie, give me back my Hershey bar."

Mother Bonita caught Eddie reading a comic book and escorted him by the ear to the back of the church, for guidance.

We suddenly acquired the spiritual look of the innocent. Who me? Incoherent, unaware of the meaning of the spoken word, we assumed our default position. We knew our nun captors also went to confession, and like referees, they had to see the foul committed before they blew the whistle. We now held the advantage.

The girls' side of the church was almost without penitents with only three girls still kneeling, waiting for their opportunity to go to confession. The boys lagged significantly behind with two pews still awaiting confession. Did girls prepare better for confession than boys? Did girls speak more succinctly than boys? Or could it have been that we boys sinned more than girls?

Girls observed who entered the confessional and how long she remained. The shorter the time in confession and doing penance the holier the penitent, marked as a person to emulate. Boys also monitored who was in the confessional and how long he spent in there, but our standards differed from the girls. The longer the time in the confessional and completing penance the greater the admiration. "Wow, Ronnie was in there for almost five minutes. I wonder what he did." To look good to our peers, some of us felt it necessary to stretch out our confessional time. We elaborated on our sins, asking questions of the confessor, requesting he repeat his comments. "I'm sorry, Father. I wasn't paying attention. Can you repeat that?" Boys may have sinned confessing their sins, becoming perpetual penitents.

Our parents supported our teachers and their judgments without question. On occasion, a nun found it necessary to send a note to my parents, indicating my deportment needed some improvement. Mom opened the note and began to read it. I watched her facial expression and began mentally composing excuses, but no opportunity presented itself to defend my position. Mom's open hand came out of nowhere, swatting me, anywhere she could make contact. She never questioned the credibility of a note from a nun; it was the "Word of God." Whenever I took home a note, which was frequently, I knew the outcome but not the severity. Mom gave Dad the note as soon as he got home from work. My father quickly read it, and his hand, much thicker and quicker than Mom's, descended upon me. Eight years of grade school seemed like an eternity.

High school spared me from this ritual. Xavier High School on Seventeenth Street in New York City was a Jesuit military prep school. Discipline was administered by the school through after-school detention and reduction in rank. I easily covered my detentions—"Traffic was bad," "We needed to take the subway and missed the first train," "Had to checkout some books at the library," or "Our practice ran over." The school failed to inform my parents about the importance of the rank a student held and that a reduction in rank indicated the seriousness of his offense. Xavier incorrectly assumed my parents understood; they had no idea. Dad, responsible for supporting his parents since he was twelve and then his family, never spent time in the service, and had no idea what the respective ranks were and what they meant. My loving mom spent several nights ripping off sergeant's stripes and sewing on corporal's then private's stripes, not knowing if that was a good or bad sign. I managed to keep up Mom's sewing skills into my senior year, graduating as a buck sergeant due to many philosophical altercations with classmates who came from a world far different from mine.

⊞

Our neighborhood stores provided the barest of essentials. To shop for clothes, appliances, furniture, and even some everyday items that the local stores did not stock, we had to leave the neighborhood. Most of us were not comfortable shopping outside the familiar blocks. We believed in supporting neighborhood businesses, knew the owners, and felt at home in these shops. Without a family escort, the neighborhood was the only place for a seven-year-old to shop.

With Mother's Day a week away, I was searching the neighborhood stores for a present for Mom. The only affordable and somewhat suitable present I found was a six-inch, gray ceramic pig. I wrapped the pig in tissue paper, tying the paper with a red-and-white pastry-shop string, and presented it to Mom with a card I had made at school. In my excitement, I dropped the present, breaking the pig's leg. Dad carefully glued the pieces together. Mom proudly placed the pig in a position of honor on top of the white metal cabinet in the kitchen together with previous inhabitants, a statue of Saint Anthony and an artificial flower in a narrow brown vase. The poor pig endured more injuries, never fully recovering from its first. Unstable, it fell several times from its perch, suffering other broken parts, many due to my hasty brushing past the cabinet in our small kitchen. The pig presently inhabits a place in our great room bookcase, side by side with pottery made by local artists, providing a source for a broad grin every day.

As an alternative to venturing out of our neighborhood to buy clothes, we could make purchases from door-to-door salespersons. Many times a neighborhood resident knocked on the apartment door at ten at night with a cardboard box full of shirts. The salesmen would say, "Vera, for you, three of these beautiful shirts for the kid. For five bucks, you can't go wrong." Vera bought the shirts, gray, blue, and white, with a red diagonal covering half the pocket. No one ever asked where anything sold door-to-door in the neighborhood came from, but we all knew.

The next day, I woke up early, grabbed my Spaldeen, and ran down the stairs to play with my friends in my new shirt. I stopped on the stoop. All the guys on Sullivan Street were wearing gray, blue, or white shirts with a red diagonal covering half the pocket. We had a neighborhood uniform!

Obtaining appliances required a different tactic. When we needed a new refrigerator, Mom first asked at the café to have the neighborhood refrigerator sales representative and supplier visit the apartment. He came after nine at night. My parents sat at the kitchen table, discussing their needs. The representative told Mom, "Vera, go to Macy's or Gimbels. Write down the make and model number of the refrigerator you want, including the price and sales tax. We always charge half or less of the store's price plus sales tax. This is due to our low overhead, your down payment, and how quickly you place the order. If you want a color other than white, we will require a delivery time beyond two weeks." The refrigerator arrived a week and half later on the weekend. Warranties were never mentioned; extended warranties were non-existent.

Graduating from high school, I received a one-year performance renewable scholarship from a neighborhood organization. The entire family supported my going to college. I would be the first. I chose a college as far from the neighborhood as possible to minimize the neighborhood's influences. Staying in the neighborhood and studying to succeed in college would have challenged my will power beyond its capacity. At seventeen, I set out for Seattle University, thirty-three hundred miles from Sullivan Street. My parents never said a negative word, although my decision must have shocked them. Their only son, leaving for a year to a place no one had been to or heard of. My parents did not have a car, never traveling outside of New York City except to see family on Staten Island or Long Island. Subway and bus routes and schedules restricted their trips. When they traveled outside of the familiar routes, a family member usually escorted them. With tears flowing down her cheeks, Mom hugged me, saying, "Do good," never questioning my decision.

Aunts and uncles came to our apartment to say goodbye the weekend before I left for college. At dinner, a discussion in which I did not participate centered on whether I should become a doctor or lawyer. The Head Aunt proclaimed, "It would be good for the family to have a doctor; we are all getting older." Authoritatively providing advice on subjects without knowledge or experience or consultation of the one involved was a common practice in our family.

After the relatives left, Mom was alone washing the dishes. The kitchen window was open to the brick airshaft with the clothes drying on the clothesline strung from the window frame. I walked over, beginning to dry dishes, and asked, "Ma, if you could choose, what would you want me to be when I graduate?" She continued washing the dishes, turned, and said, "Don't be a bum. Be you. Be responsible, not dependent. You decide; it's your life." She wiped wet hands on her apron and gave me a hug and kiss. Neither of us realized that night how long the next ten months would be.

Arriving home from Seattle after my first year at one a.m., I stood in the building entryway and pressed the bell to Apartment #64. Within seconds, the buzzer activated to open the entrance door. Mom excitedly met me halfway on the third floor landing, waking many neighbors in the process. Dad and Papa John, previously asleep, sat at the kitchen table, anxiously awaiting my appearance. Once I had entered the kitchen, Dad officially called the meeting to order, asking, "When did you leave? How did you get home? Do you like the school?" I answered his questions while Mom set out cookies, biscotti, *tarallis*, and wine.

Dad continued questioning after eating a cookie, "How did you do in school? Did you pass?"

I smiled, proudly saying, "My GPA is 2.84!"

The response met with blank stares and silence. Seeing my smile, the audience assumed the response meant all was well, together responding, "Good, good." Papa John then said with a smile, "*Bene.*" Only letter grades As, Bs, Cs, and Ds had meaning in their world. My parents never asked about deportment, thank God.

The next morning, I was standing on the corner of Spring and Sullivan Streets, getting an update on current neighborhood news. We were on the sidewalk outside of Carmine's grocery store, Rocco, Marro, Mikie "Smash," Petey D, Ronnie "Patch," and Petey "Rags." My mother's cousin from Thompson Street, Magdalene, was returning from morning shopping when she saw me on the corner. She immediately stopped, put down her two shopping bags, and walked directly into the group. Grabbing my arm and pulling me aside, she said, "Good to see you out. I hope and pray you'll go straight."

Magdalene knew no one left the neighborhood by choice. Being gone for a year meant one of two things—either I had been drafted, or I had spent time upstate in a correctional facility. Magdalene knew I was not in the Army.

Over the next four years, I managed to return home when school was over in June and, thanks to part-time jobs at school, at Christmas as well. I easily slipped back into the familiar Sullivan Street. But the transition from New York City to Seattle was difficult for a city kid homesick for the neighborhood. Adjusting to my new environment proved difficult; the chip I carried on my shoulder did not help, leading to several discussions with the dean of students. After a late-night discussion with Father Rebhahn, the next day, Dick Cavaliere, a student, showed up at my door in the dorm. Dick, Italian and a junior, came from Schenectady, New York. With Dick's mentoring, my deportment improved, and I received the gift of a friend and brother for life.

Academics at the college level did not come easy for me. I had to work hard, putting in long hours for passing grades. Even taking summer classes, I took five years to graduate. Finally, I achieved the family's dream, the first college graduate. Overwhelmed by good fortune, the gray horse, the long shot, finished by a nose and graduated thanks to all the prayers and candles lit by Mom, aunts, and cousins for five years. I had reason to celebrate, as did all the important people in my life. Yet the two who had made it all possible did not join me in my celebration. And, yes, I was disappointed. But Mom and Dad's universe did not encompass Seattle. How could they understand, based on their experience, what graduation meant, let alone my desires? They had already worked the miracle—given up everything for me and trusted the judgment of a seventeen-year-old so that I could realize *my* dream. Nothing more did I need.

No matter how far apart, how infrequent my letters, Mom sent a letter once every week, birthday and holiday cards, a care package three to four times a year. Cards and letters included a crisp five-dollar bill and stamps, a hint. Mom continued this tradition with her grandchildren, sending packages before holidays stuffed with clothes, Italian foods, cheese, and desserts not available in Seattle. The smell of mothballs and cheese transported me back to childhood and the comfort of Apartment #64.

Mom, together with aunts and cousins, continued this practice when I was in the army. Away from our base camp in Vietnam for two weeks, I was anxious to pick up my mail. Mail was stored in a Conex container at the ammo dump. The sergeant in charge approached, asking, "What's up captain?"

"I'd like my mail."

He took a quick look at the nametag on the faded jungle fatigues, smiled, and, turning to a young private, said, "Morris, get your ass down to Conex B and get Captain Vivolo's mail."

Morris took off in a jeep, burning rubber, spewing gravel around us. Conex B, covered with sand bags, was at the rear of the dump, far from the bunker. Morris returned, placing before me a package covered with oily brown paper and smelling so bad my face became the color of my fatigues. I quickly signed for the mail under the sergeant's smirk and loaded it in the jeep as I heard Morris in the background say, "I'm so frigging happy to get that goddamn box out of our C-4 area. We need to find someone else to handle this mail shit."

Mom had sent a Christmas package with all sorts of wonderful foods—a white mold-covered, dry *sopressata*, a large piece of moldy blue Locatelli, a piece of moldy green provolone, and nondescript pieces of Italian pastries. Laughing, I put a piece of dry candy in my mouth, depositing the remaining portion of the package into a burn barrel while continuing to sip on the bottle of red wine.

My favorite holiday growing up was Christmas Eve. Family, neighbors, and friends gathered around Aunt Rosie's big table. Loud voices together with loud laughter exploded at the table. Christmas Day was somewhat of a letdown, even with the presents. Families tended to be alone with fewer visitors spending less time laughing and sharing stories. The Christmas Eve meal was always elaborate by our standards and meatless. Mom served baked calamari stuffed with breadcrumbs, eggs, cheese, onions, parsley, and garlic with a marinara tentacle sauce served over a bed of linguini. Dad ate only the pasta and sauce since he did not eat fish. Growing up, I had this special meal only once a year, although every time I visited from college, the Army, or with my family, stuffed calamari always found their way onto the menu, the dish presented as a gift of love to its recipients.

Although my parents didn't attend my graduation from college, they did witness our marriage. Pat and I called Mom and Dad, telling of our future wedding plans, and after many rosaries and novenas, my parents decided to make their first trip to Seattle for the wedding. Their tour guide, the Head Aunt, provided the courage to leave New York City and navigate this unknown world. Subways, buses, and cabs were the only trusted methods of travel for my folks. The Vivolo-Greco expedition, amply equipped with clothes, Italian provisions, and cash set out for the Northwest by train. Navigating the turbulent Chicago train station in a snowstorm, finding the path to the *Empire Builder*, and fending off the Chicago natives with cash, they slowly proceeded west through snow, ice, and wind to their destination. The Northwest natives, members of the bride's tribe, met the Vivolo -Greco expedition. After an exchange of hugs, kisses, and gifts the Vivolo-Greco party settled into their new campsite, the first hotel my parents had stayed in since their wedding. Aunt Helen may not have been on my parents' honeymoon, but she was here now.

We had a simple wedding. It was 1968, and most of our close friends were in the service or the Peace Corps. I was in the Army at the time, and our honeymoon coincided with my ten-day leave. After the ceremony, the Vivolo-Greco party found its way, without Italian provisions but with souvenirs of Seattle, back to New York City.

We had our first child, their first grandchild, Laura. Wrapping our six-month-old in a pink snowsuit, we traveled to New York for our family's "show and tell." Held, cherished, and oohed and aahed over by the family, our "Wonderful Gift" received the usual overwhelming abundance of Italian love. We spent several days visiting relatives and friends, and at the end of each day of the visit, after first addressing Laura's needs, a mandatory meeting convened at the kitchen table. We discussed the day's events, how everyone looked, how special this day was, and expressed sorrow that family members who had died were not present to see this "Wonderful Gift."

Mom asked, "Are you hungry?" The tradition in every Italian household calls for filling visitors with food from the first moment of stepping over the threshold to the last moment in departing. To decline from eating each special dish insults the host. Visitors have no choice but to eat and try everything presented, giving due honor to the cook for the days—not hours—spent in preparation.

We knew the rules, but after spending the entire day visiting, eating, and drinking with family we answered with a resounding, "No!"

Mom stepped slightly back from the response, saying, "OK, I will make some coffee." She went to the sink, filling the coffee pot, then added the grounds and placed it on the stove. Undeterred by our answer, Mom interrupted our discussion at the table and said, "While we wait for the water to boil, pick on some of these cookies and pastries I bought this morning."

I was released from the army in 1970. Pat and I had our second child, Joe, the following year. Visiting New York now presented more problems with two children, limited space, and limited funds. Two years later after the birth of our third child, Annemarie, the Vivolo-Greco expedition set off again for the Northwest, this excursion by car. Cousin Gilda and her husband, Jimmy, drove the five-party expedition from New York to Bothell, Washington. Dad had never ridden in a car for a long period. Anxious and having to relinquish control for three thousand miles, he never repeated the trip by car.

Dad was a cautious man, and although he never had a driver's license, he knew the proper speed to travel for the road conditions. According to him, fifty miles an hour was an excessive speed. He also provided guidance on how much distance to maintain to the car ahead. "You're getting too close. Are you trying to kill us?" Dad also knew the shortest route to take to the next city although he had never been there. He sat in the back seat, clinging to his armrest, looking out at the world passing by, his head spinning. Dad was sitting in the rollercoaster at Coney Island, not in a car traveling seventy-five miles an hour in Iowa.

During the journey, the expedition spent much time discussing food and places to stay; sightseeing was not on their agenda. Where to spend the night was a great concern for all the members. Gilda and Jimmy, worldlier and younger, became the decision-makers. Regardless of cost, location, and assurances, every room received "the assault" from three Italian women with exceptional housekeeping skills and expectations. The door unlocked, Gilda, the youngest, entered first with a can of disinfectant, spraying from room to room, then opening drawers and spraying into each. Helen pulled down all the bedspreads and blankets looking for "visitors." Mom went into the bathroom, pulling back shower curtains, running the water, and repeating the process on the sink and toilet. Once the "all clear" sounded, Jimmy and Dad carried in the suitcases and shopping bags.

The expedition arrived in Bothell. We fed the group, let them bathe, and gave them several hours to rest before participating in the ceremony of the presentation of the gifts. Custom dictated that the youngest receive the first gift and so on with the oldest last. After Laura opened her last present, Mom indicated it was now Pat's turn. She presented my wife with the bounty of the spoils of the expedition—a mixture of restaurant forks, knives, spoons, salt and peppershakers, and shiny metal sugar and cream dispensers. Pat's face displayed her astonishment. Mom recognized the look and said, "It's not that much; they will never miss it. Here are some more things." The Head Aunt now presented a large stack of white bath and hand towels, boldly emblazoned with a green band and the words "Holiday Inn."

Several years later, we took the children on a vacation to Eastern Washington where they could swim and play in the hot sunny climate. We carried the bags to the room, unpacking while the kids hurriedly changed for the pool. As we settled into our poolside lounges, Joe with his five-year-old outdoor voice observed, "Mom, Dad, they have towels just like ours!"

My parents and Aunt Helen stayed at our three-bedroom house for two months. Jimmy and Gilda left after a week to visit a cousin in California. I often wonder if, instead, they went straight back to Staten Island to get a good night's sleep. Our house was an old farm-house with a menagerie of two- and four-legged animals. Our lifestyle and furnishings contrasted sharply with that of Sullivan Street. Aunt Helen, raised on a farm near Genoa, felt perfectly comfortable in her new surroundings as did Mom. Dad definitely did not. Feeding and watering farm animals, being in woods of tall cedar and fir, having unfamiliar plants all around, magnified dad's fear, knowing the foliage provided hiding places for things that bite, sting, and give no warning of an attack. He was comfortable only in the house or on the concrete patio and asphalt driveway. Mom was happy anywhere her children and grandchildren were.

We attempted to show off our Northwest, taking the expedition to areas of the state we thought demonstrated its beauty and, in turn, why we had elected to live here. Our visitors were city people. "Once you see one tree and one mountain, you've seen them all," summed up their response to our sightseeing attempts. Frustrated, we changed our approach, asking our visitors what they wanted to see. If we received limited responses, we provided suggestions. Finally, everyone was having their needs met, making the visit a success. The last week of the stay approached, and Pat said, "Mom, you haven't said what you would like to see or do. Would you like to go to the theater? Go to a play or symphony or an art museum?"

Glancing shyly at Pat, Mom said, "I'd like to go to the track."

The next day we headed to Longacres Racetrack to handicap the ponies. Mom practiced the neighborhood's tried and true approach to betting horses: "Always bet the gray horse and say a silent prayer to Saint Jude," patron saint of lost articles. Barring a gray, bets went based on the color of the silks, the horse's number in the race, and most important, the name of the horse. Bets were always made well before the parade to post. "You don't need to see the horses to bet on them."

"And they're off!" triggered laughter, excitement, and cheers for our four-legged friends. Mom cashed in several winners, much to the dismay of the two handicappers sitting behind us, who eventually changed seats.

The visit ended, and they left. Seeing their grandchildren, hearing their voices, watching them play, living with dogs, cats, goat, sheep, geese, chickens, pony, the house and woods would not happen tomorrow, but now they could shut their eyes and replay their visit.

Six years later, the Vivolo-Greco expedition arrived by train, experienced and confident, with few provisions. The kids and house were older, so were we, and we decided to take a trip to the Oregon Coast, a place where we vacationed with our children for most summers, wanting to share that experience with my parents and the Head Aunt.

Piling into a ten-year-old Volkswagen van, five adults, three children, and Daisy, the dog, we took off. Above the whine of the Volkswagen's engine, we told stories, clapped hands, sang, and described the scenes from the van's windows. We played alphabetical car bingo—players looked out their window and had to find an item starting with the letter selected. The first player seeing and describing it received a point; the most points acquired won the game. The letters Q, X, and Z provided soothing periods of silence. We stopped several times, consuming foods that should not be in anyone's diet. At the end of eight hours, our taste buds destroyed, we arrived at Cannon Beach, Oregon, laughing and singing. We stayed at the Surf Sand Hotel in two units with kitchens, one for us and one for the expedition. Mom and Dad referred to theirs as "our rooms," a term of endearment they both used all their lives to describe their apartment on Sullivan Street. Spending time at a place where they could walk outside onto a beach with the ocean at their feet was something they had never experienced. My last memory of our trip is of Mom and Helen, in house dresses, shoes in one hand, holding each other's hands, walking barefoot in the water, laughing and giggling.

Dad called the day before Thanksgiving less than a year later. Mom was in the hospital with breast cancer. Flying back that night, I was able to arrive before Dad met with her surgeon and oncologist. The cancer had spread, the tumor was large, and her breast would have to be removed. After the doctors left, I asked, "Did Mom have yearly checkups?"

"Every year she had one."

I wondered how this could happen, her tumor being so large. We never received an adequate explanation, but one would not have made a difference.

The tumor removed, Mom was released from the hospital and transported to Apartment #64. We arranged for a health aide, and with Dad's assurance, I told myself things in the future would improve. Speaking on the phone, Mom played the healthy and happy person. All was going well; she had returned to shopping for herself and cooking. "Don't worry about me. How are the children?" Dad's tone of voice did not sound as encouraging.

In January, Mom went back to the hospital. Mom was in pain; the cancer had spread to her bones. Pat and I flew back, finding Mom barely coherent on pain medication, drifting in and out of reality. Conversations with her oncologist together with her prognosis led us to look at nursing homes for her care after release from the hospital. The more we looked the more difficult it was to be positive. We visited several places, and Dad's expression of hopelessness and the thought of Mom living in such an environment frightened me as much as anything I had witnessed in Vietnam.

Reality set in, and we selected a hospice facility to transfer her to on her release from the hospital. We arranged support for Dad, contacting Aunt Helen, Rosemary, Gloria, and Aunt Rosie for daily and weekly visits. After spending another week, we left for Seattle. Dad received daily phone calls, and aunts and cousins visited as frequently as possible after our departure.

Mom never left the hospital. Two weeks later, I received the anticipated call from Dad at work. With tears streaming down my face, I grabbed my coat, walked to the front desk, and said, "My mommy died; I need to go home."

I think of Mom every day. I have no tears in my eyes or heart, only smiles, laughter, and wonderment. I was blessed. My mom was my "Wonderful Gift."

Ode to Stuffed Squid

Squid on ice, tentacles and tails,
Bodies white with purple tails,
Sliding through wet hands,
These slippery slick skins.

Where do they come from?
How do you catch them?
What do you do with them?
How much do you pay for them?

When told about them,
I could not behold
Someone caught them
To be so cheaply sold.

How do you cook something so cheap?
Really, are they good enough to eat?
Remove clear cartilage from tail.
Tentacles, tails, into cold-water pail.

Pondering what to do
With this purple goo,
From far away,
I hear Mom say,

"Brown garlic in olive oil,
"Onions, tomatoes, oregano.
"Separate heads from tails.
"Heads, tentacles into sauce.

"Loosely stuff tiny tails,
"Breadcrumbs, garlic, parsley,
"Eggs, cheese, and celery.
"Sew together carefully.

"Slowly simmer tentacle sauce.
"Bake stuffed tails in sauce.
"Cover linguini thoroughly
"With sauce, tentacles, and tails.

"Bravo, Bravo."
It is Christmas Eve
Fifty years ago.
Grazie, Mamma, saluti.

Mom and Dad in front of 120 Sullivan Street

Dad

Antonio Vivolo, born in 1909, was the younger of two children. Dad was smart, always serious, proper, and responsible. Neighborhood friends would tell him, "Relax Tony! Have some fun." Dad graduated from grade school, skipping seventh grade, and got a job sweeping floors and cleaning up a machine shop. Three months later, this twelve-year-old accepted an offer of a full-time job as an apprentice, making more money than his dad did as a barber. He became the breadwinner for the family, casting aside any plans to go to high school. He told us many times how he wished he had had that opportunity, making education a mantra in our apartment.

During the Depression, Dad was the primary wage earner for his immediate family, other family members, and friends in need. Responsible as a son, husband, and father, working long hours every day, doing odd jobs, he put family first. No one smiled, raised a glass of wine, and said, "Hey Tony! Be more serious, be more responsible!"

Some of the men in our neighborhood did not commend long-term employment but placed more emphasis on avoiding steady jobs. Bragging rights went to those who never worked a regular job but always made money, somehow. When I met Pat, I proudly revealed, "My dad has a job and goes to work every day." She wondered, "What is with this guy?

Every man I know has a job." Only after visiting Sullivan Street did she understand how my father stood out from the rest in his work ethic.

Mom's personality, sense of humor, and joy of life naturally and easily drew me to her. In grade school, things slowly began to change. After a week of ten- and twelve-hour workdays, Dad sometimes had Saturday off, and it became our day together. We took a bus from Washington Square up Fifth Avenue to Central Park. Although outside his familiar world, the park felt safe for Dad, perhaps because he had visited it on a grade-school field trip. Now it was my turn to explore a new world where people lived, dressed, and spoke differently. The buildings were unlike those in our neighborhood. Many rose only three stories high; others, wider and higher, had men in uniforms guarding the street-level doors.

We walked through Central Park into the zoo, stopping at each animal enclosure. Dad read to me the plaque on each exhibit, pronouncing the Latin genus and species names as best he could. Sometimes we took lunch with us; other times; we had lunch at the zoo cafeteria—a hot dog and soda for me, a hot dog and beer for Dad. In winter after visiting each exhibit, we lingered in the monkey and birdhouses to keep warm. We walked along the lake to catch the bus or subway home, stopping at the pony cart rides where sometimes I received two rides, not one.

One Saturday, we planned to go to the zoo, but the trip had to be canceled because Dad had to work. We rescheduled the trip to Sunday. Our family went to 7 a.m. mass at Saint Anthony's, the Italian mass with the mass said in Latin and the gospel, sermon, and announcements in Italian. After mass, we went back to Apartment #64, changed our clothes, grabbed a quick breakfast, and promised we would be back early for Sunday dinner. We began our adventure.

It was a sunny, windy, cold morning in late October, the sidewalks on Fifty-ninth Street filled with Sunday walkers. We walked on the south side of Fifty-ninth Street adjacent to the expensive apartments and hotels; the horse-drawn hansom cabs and Central Park were on the opposite side of the street.

A middle age man and woman walked towards us. The man wore a three-piece dark gray suit, white shirt, a blue silk tie with small

Feeding pigeons
in Central Park

On a pony cart ride in Central Park

horizontal black stripes. Over the outfit, he had on a three-quarter-length light brown camelhair coat, the dark brown collar turned up at the back of the neck. His left hand grasped a fat Sunday paper. As he walked towards us, the sun reflected off his black, pointy-toed, Italian leather shoes and cascaded off his woven gold watchband, watch, and rings. His female companion wore maroon high-heeled shoes, sheer nylon stockings, and a short, dark red silk dress showing through the unbuttoned light brown mink coat. Sunlight softly reflected off the pearl necklace and long dangling earrings. Her hand with a diamond bracelet gestured at Central Park while she laughed and smiled. Her companion was oblivious, looking in another direction.

Directly behind them in a gray uniform with gold buttons and red cap walked a man holding red leather leashes of two white Yorkshire terriers, bounding and jumping in the direction of everyone passing. The man in gray uniform was older, gray hair protruding from his red cap and absorbing, not reflecting, the sunlight. As he walked by us, the leashes slackened, and he nodded to us, a smile emerging then fading quickly as the leashes became taut.

Although dad had worked since his twelfth year, all he was paid and maybe all he would be paid for the rest of his life would not buy the clothes and jewelry this man and woman were wearing. The opulence of the buildings on Fifty-ninth Street and the people walking on it were beyond my comprehension. I still remember the look and smile of the man in uniform walking the dogs and how his employers never saw dad and me; we didn't exist in their eyes and their world.

Dad pointed to a horse-drawn carriage with a young man and woman happily sitting side-by-side, holding hands, having an animated discussion interrupted by laughter while waving to smiling passersby. The driver of the hansom cab wore a top hat, and the gray horse wore a matching one, altered to accommodate the large ears, as it proudly clomped down Fifty-ninth Street into Central Park.

As I grew older, summer trips to the zoo included visits to the model sailboats on Seventy-second Street Pond not far from a lake where you could rent a wooden rowboat by the hour. During the week, I made sailboats from scrap lumber and bent nails, complete with a rag sail, waiting for an opportunity to float my boat in the pond on Seventy-second Street alongside the fancy boats. I imagined my boat out-sailing all of the boats on the pond, finding its way back to me through a hurricane. I placed the boat onto the pond, praying a silent prayer and pushing it off. The wind came up, and the boat traveled to the center of the pond, never to return to shore.

The rowboat, thanks to Dad's ability, always returned to shore and always within an hour. On the rowboat, I learned how to fish, using heavy black thread and a bent safety pin as a hook. I took Wonder bread from my lunch, added some water, and rolled it into a small ball, which I applied to the safety-pin hook. I caught my first fish, a two-inch sunfish, eventually working my way up to a trophy fish exceeding four inches.

Sometimes fishing and sailing model boats didn't happen; my sandwich crusts then fed pigeons, squirrels, and sometimes just me. If I had any allowance left or if one of my aunts or uncles rewarded me, I bought pony food. The ponies were sloppy eaters, spilling most of the food from my small hands onto the ground where the squirrels and pigeons feasted, much as they did with my sandwich crusts.

As I grew older, our trips to the zoo sometimes wound up at a museum or the Cloisters. On our bus trips home, we stopped on Broadway and Forty-second Street or at Macy's or Gimbels on Thirty-fourth Street. Taking the subway, we exited at Chambers Street, walking past old churches, through cemeteries, reading tombstone names and dates. In the huge city, Dad and I wandered alone, not a soul in sight; it was the weekend, and no one worked during the weekend even in the financial district.

If the weather was mild, we walked from Central Park down Fifth or Sixth Avenue to Forty-second Street; people watching, just killing time. In summer, we bought hot dogs and soda; in winter, roasted chestnuts while we watched the ice skaters at Rockefeller Center under the largest Christmas tree in the city. Dad gave me an education outside of grade school much as he did for himself, enjoying learning for learning's sake.

Dad was the go-to guy in 120 Sullivan Street for repairing mechanical and electrical equipment and appliances. At the time, no one in the neighborhood considered appliance repair a viable occupation. We had few appliances, all well designed and manufactured to last forever. Dad repaired radios and televisions using a self-help book, titled *Radio and Television Repair*. He removed odd-shaped tubes, taking them to the hardware store for testing. Replacing tubes, soldering wires, putting up new antennas, he somehow managed to get things to work. I watched him perform his magic but with no desire to imitate him in this realm. Not having his patience or mechanical ability, I gravitated to physical jobs, content with testing strength rather than mind.

Having a small apartment for five people with limited space and much shared area, dad kept all his tools and equipment in one drawer and a wooden box. Sometimes, I would borrow a tool, carefully clean and replace it. Prior to borrowing it, I recorded on paper its exact location, using tape measure records. Dad returned from work, opened the drawer, and immediately inquired, "Who has been in my drawer using my pliers?"

How he knew, I never determined. Maybe he plucked a hair from his head, putting it on the top of the drawer edge or under each piece of equipment, as in the old black-and-white detective movies. Dad did not have much hair, but he knew, he always knew and was right.

Dad worked on Hudson and Varrick Streets, seven blocks from our apartment, for over forty-five years. He began his employment working in the machine shop, next onto the telephone assembly line, and finally as an inspector checking the work of others. He had his breakfast at five thirty and by six was out the door, walking to work at Western Electric. I never remember him staying home from work, even when sick. During heavy snowstorms with over two feet of snow, Dad put cardboard in his shoes, pulled on rubber boots, filled the boots with newspaper extending up his leg, and finally wrapped the top of the newspaper with masking tape, ready to began his trek.

I always found summer jobs on my own—hauling groceries and stocking shelves at Cardinali's grocery store, doing yard maintenance at New York City's housing project on Houston and Avenue D, loading and unloading trucks at Walsh Trucking, painting apartments, cleaning out basements, whatever it took, as long as it took. The year I graduated from high school, Dad encouraged me to apply for a job at

Western Electric. No way did I want to work with Dad, but the pay, if I got the job, was better than anything I could find. Unaccompanied, I went to Western Electric for the interview, filled out the application, interviewed, and left. I had a good but not great interview and hoped for success. I was apprehensive about working around Dad but really wanted the money. Dad never asked about the interview or if I got the job. A week later the job was mine, and Dad was happy when I told him the news.

We went to work at different times, came home at different times, only seeing each other twice at work in two and a half months. My job involved cleaning restrooms, mucking out storage areas, once a day cleaning and sweeping the loading dock together with the warehouse area adjacent to it. The warehouse cut communications wire, rolled and stacked it on pallets for construction crews. Later in summer, I got to work in the warehouse.

After a hot humid day of work, covered in dirt and sweat, having spent the day cleaning out an elevator shaft, I stopped at Aunt Rosie's on my way up to our apartment. Rosie looked at me with that twinkle in those dark brown eyes, shook her head, and said with a smile, "So how do you like your job?"

It was not a time to ask that question. I unloaded my frustrations on her. "All I get are the lousiest, dirtiest jobs. Most of the time, I work alone. I don't know if I'm doing good or bad or what. Nobody really gives a shit."

Unbeknownst to me, Dad was in the living room, stopping on his way upstairs to have a beer with his sister. He entered the kitchen, looked at me, and said, "I give a shit since my name is attached to your performance, whether you give a shit or not." He turned, heading back to the living room. I knew I had crossed the line; no one valued a good reputation more than Dad did. I apologized later that night.

Saint Anthony's Church constructed a Memorial Hall with a gym, stage, and meeting rooms, which the parish and neighborhood used. Heading to the gym for basketball one day, we saw a boxing ring assembled in the gym.

Each of us thought he was the next Rocky Marciano, I more so than most since Uncle Joe gave me boxing lessons when I was little and I still remembered what he had taught me. We guys signed up, received instructions, paired by weight and age, and into the ring we went. Despite my previous pugilistic training, I learned two things—three rounds last an extremely long, long time, and I really did not know how to box. After putting wet toilet paper up my left nostril for half an hour, the bleeding stopped, the lip took a little longer, and the bruised eye got bigger instead of smaller. Licking my wounds, I headed up the stairs to our apartment. I entered the kitchen. Dad looked up, put down his *New York Daily News*, and stared at me. Quickly I said, "I was at the Memorial Hall. They set up a boxing ring, and I learned how to box."

Dad paused, inspecting me with intense brown eyes, and said, "I can see that." These four words were the only comments he ever made about any of the sports I played. Dad was a man of few words but he was succinct.

When it came to a discussion on food, Dad found more words. He was a man of consistency, of the familiar, and loved all food except anything green, anything that swam in fresh or salt water, and anything classified as a fruit, unless it was in a pastry. Dad's idea of a healthy breakfast consisted of a cup of coffee with strawberry shortcake or an Italian pastry. At lunch, Italian cold cuts and Italian bread but never mayonnaise. "You know, it's got raw eggs in it."

Dad never ate a green salad or seafood. Being Catholic and preparing a meatless dinner each Friday to please everyone proved challenging to my mother. As a teenager, I ate lunch many times in the neighborhood or at school. I began eating canned tuna fish with dill pickles and mayonnaise, all of which were on my father's non-edible list. Mom also enjoyed a good tuna fish sandwich, making them in the kitchen when only she and I were present, knowing she was, in Dad's perception, committing a mortal sin.

During a rainy summer Friday, we both had our tuna fish sandwiches and played some gin. The rain ceased, and I headed to the street.

Dad and me on
Staten Island

Our Miracle on
34th Street

Mom put the leftover tuna fish in a soup dish, placing a salad plate on top as a cover, into the refrigerator. Dad came home from work, and after a brief discussion, he placed his newspaper on the table, taking a beer out of the refrigerator. He stopped at the door of the refrigerator. Raising the cold beer to his nose, he turned quickly, facing us and saying in his best Sherlock Holmes voice, "I can smell fish!"

Mom and I put on our best choirboy expression in facing Dad's inquisition, Papa John's stogie smoldering in the background. We innocently smelled the prosecution's Exhibit A, the suspect beer can, declaring, "We can't smell anything." Dad stood erect, Exhibit B, the incriminating evidence, in his hand, a wide grin on his face. He knew a crime when he smelled one—Holmes had found the culprits—and he gingerly removed the evil tuna from the refrigerator. How could dad bait fishing hooks, removing fish from hooks, and put the fish back into Central Park Lake and have this reaction to a can of tuna fish?

During my parent's first trip to Seattle, I wanted my father to see why I had left the neighborhood, choosing to live far from Sullivan Street. Our house was in the woods, an old farmhouse on two and a half acres. On the first night of their visit, I asked Pat to turn off all the lights. I took Dad by the hand outside. We stood in the black silent yard, and after several minutes I proudly said, "Look at this, look at this. Isn't it beautiful?"

He looked around, slowly turning, and said, "What? What? I don't see a goddamn thing."

Laughing, I said, "Yeah, isn't it beautiful?"

He shook his head and retreated cautiously into the safety of our house as the lights quickly came on.

We teamed up on several projects during that visit. I worked on replacing our cedar shake roof; he worked at repairing lamps and small appliances and replacing the webbing on all our aluminum lawn chairs. The work necessitated frequent trips to the hardware store with my four-year-old son and a stop at the ice cream parlor across the street. I don't know if the stop at the ice cream parlor was for my son or my dad.

After dinner, the grandchildren sat down with Grandma and Grandpa for their lesson in five-card stud poker. Mom bet on anything, never folding her hand. She believed in the power of prayer and faith along with a pinch of salt over her left shoulder and a dance three times counterclockwise around her chair before sitting down. Dad, on the other hand, stuck with the odds. A realist, he played poker in the neighborhood for real money. "Fold if you don't have anything. Remember every card played. Mentally re-calculate the odds for your hand." Dad could play the game only by those rules. The grandchildren remember Grandma teaching them to play poker. "Grandpa didn't like poker that much; he only played half the games."

My father lived in the shadow of his wife who was as extroverted as he was introverted. He was always there for the family and me, always supportive, shunning attention, preferring the background. Only after Mom died did I really get to know and bond with Dad. Maybe, too, I was now mature enough to see what I didn't see earlier.

Mom died in April, and in September, Rosemary called; Dad was in Saint Vincent's Hospital with a bleeding ulcer. I left that same day on a redeye flight from Seattle, dropped my bag off at Aunt Rosie's apartment, and went to the hospital. I spoke to Dad's doctor. The ulcer was treated, and the bleeding had stopped. However, Dad had lost a significant amount of blood. He was receiving intravenous liquids and remained sedated from the procedure. The doctor said, "He should be up and about by this evening."

Walking into Dad's room, I stopped and backed into the door, sensing I was in Uncle Jimmy's funeral parlor. In bed with arms folded over his chest, eyes closed, no sign of movement was my father. "Dad, it's me. I'm here. How are you?"

The eyelids slowly rose, a quarter of the pupil now showing, and his head slowly turned in my direction. Then in his best B movie imitation, he said, "Is that you? Come closer so I can see you."

"The doctor didn't say anything about your losing your eyesight or your voice. He did say once you are rehydrated and get some sleep you will be fine."

"I don't know about that." The conversation ceased. His eyes closed, and he resumed the position of the dead.

Silently, I began structuring my opening statement, wondering how best to approach this jury without alienating him. I needed to gain his trust in this most important discussion about to follow. Faltering with my opening statement, I began several times, "Dad, we need to talk." "Dad, where do we go from here?" "Dad, what do you want?" All of which were met with closed eyes and no response. I paced. Finally, I presented my closing argument to this jury of one.

"Dad, I think you have some decisions to make. Let's start with the best alternative. You can leave here, have a health aide a few days a week until you can handle things on your own, and go back to your apartment. Or you can come out to Seattle and be with us. If you can't take care of yourself, you can go to a nursing home here or in Seattle. The worst choice is to fold your hands, close your eyes, give up, and die. Think about these choices and any others you have in mind. I'm going to get a cup of coffee then come back, and we'll talk." I left the room. The jury was now sequestered.

Returning after twenty minutes, I opened the door. Dad's eyes now fully open, he greeted me—"Hey, kid, how are yah doing? It's good to see you"—as if I had just arrived and the previous half-hour had never occurred. I sat on the edge of the bed and held his hands. We talked for over an hour. We discussed our concerns, fears, what we could do now, what comes next, what both of us expect.

Dad was now ready to go back to "his rooms"—no longer "their rooms"— beginning a new phase of his life at seventy-five.

During one of many telephone calls, Pat suggested I contact the discharge planner prior to Dad leaving the hospital. We arranged for visits from a health aide, diet, physical therapy, and an assessment of the apartment for safety aids. Once Dad was comfortably settled in the apartment, I went out to do some shopping. I filled the refrigerator, stocked the freezer, and outfitted the pantry and cupboards with cans and boxes of food, creating a sight that would have brought smiles from Mom and Aunt Helen.

I made Dad *pastina in brodo* with chicken and egg, knowing it was not only his favorite but nutritious, possessing spiritual and medicinal benefits.

Dad adjusted to his new life, going out every morning to shop, in the afternoon visiting friends in the park on Sixth Avenue and Prince Street. He always stopped at his sister's, now having a soda. "I quit beer after my bleeding ulcer." Dad cooked most of the time, with a very limited menu. Breakfast was a poached egg, toast, or cereal; lunch a sandwich; dinner a hamburger. Substitutions did occur; Italian pastry always fit into the menu along with ice cream or Jell-O. Dad was making significant changes. Not only did he shop and cook for himself, but "green" entered his diet. Arriving early one visit, I interrupted his dinner. There on the table was a hamburger on a bun with catsup and green relish.

Upon visiting, I placed my luggage on the living room linoleum. We held hands after a hug and kiss and headed for the kitchen. Once seated with a glass of red wine and a soda for Dad, court was in session. "What's new? What's going on in Seattle? How are the kids?" I then conducted a visual inspection of the refrigerator and pantry. We discussed his daily life and his needs the next morning over coffee and Entenmann's coffeecake. I cleaned the apartment, washing floors and windows, polishing, and dusting. We had lunch at the kitchen table with sandwiches of my favorite Italian cold cuts that Dad proudly presented and dinner most nights at Porto Bello on Thompson Street.

We walked different streets to the restaurant and back to his apartment. "Remember when Aunt Annie lived in that building?' "That store used to be a bakery; now it's an antique shop. Makes sense since we're now all antiques." Many places still looked the same on the outside, but the insides were different. Growing up, we never had a Tibetan Art Boutique. We laughed, thinking who in the family would have shopped there and what they might have purchased.

Our walks from the restaurant also took different paths depending on Dad's health. One fall evening, the temperature was in the seventies, and Dad was not tired so we extended our walk. We went up Spring Street from Thompson to Sullivan. The restaurants were seating diners at the sidewalk tables. At an outside table, an attractive woman stood up and waved in our direction. She was my age, but I had no idea who she could be. She excused herself from her dinner companions, napkin in hand, and came running towards us. My mind was racing—who was this lovely woman, where did I know her from, when was the last time I had seen her? Three feet away, she spread her arms, embracing my father. Dad was always a gentleman, making friends easily with his respectful manner and smile. I stood in silence and awe, waiting for an introduction.

The building owner was in the process of remodeling apartments, converting the apartments to larger units and renting at substantial increases, well above what Dad was paying on rent control. Shortly after Aunt Rosie died, the building owner proposed moving Dad from his four-room apartment on the fifth floor to a three-room apartment on the third floor, formerly cousin Rosemary's. The monthly rent would remain the same under the terms of rent control.

Two flights of stairs were a big deal to someone his age making two to three trips per day to Sullivan Street. Leaving the memories and visions that inhabited his four rooms over the last fifty years was also a significant factor in the decision. We discussed the alternatives, leaving the decision Dad's to make. He decided to move. I flew in and with our attorney's help signed a new lease, assisting in his first move in fifty years.

Dad and I cleaned out the three-foot walk-in closet located in my grandfather's bedroom, a task never attempted when Mom died. The closet contained our family's treasured possessions. Clothes suitable to wear on important occasions, weddings, funerals, baptisms, First Communions, confirmations, important family functions, and a surprise visit from the Pope or president. In this closet, the good tablecloths and napkins, cleaned, ironed, folded, were placed on wooden hangers covered with plastic, awaited important visitors. Sheets, pillowcases, blankets, bedspreads, and some gifts from their wedding shared this precious space. To protect the possessions, mothballs placed in cloth bags hung from hooks. Some were scattered onto the floor. At any of those important occasions, the smell of mothballs overpowered perfume, incense, and garlic cooking in olive oil.

Dad carefully decided what would move to his new apartment and what was to be discarded, meticulously planning where each piece of furniture would be located. To me, merely indicating that a piece of furniture would be in the living room would have sufficed; not to Dad. He needed to know the exact location of each piece of furniture on the square-tile linoleum floor. The patterned floor became the engineer's graph paper, providing guides the former inspector used to locate each piece of furniture.

I slept in the living room as a child and adult, so every night we had to move furniture to pull out the bed from the couch. In the morning, back everything went, and then the inspection began. The yellow living room chair, the good chair, had its front feet placed on the diamond corner of the third tile from the wall and the middle of the space between the fifth and sixth tile, placed on a forty-five-degree diagonal between the tiles east and west. Dad conducted a similar ritual daily with every piece of furniture, eventually including even silverware, cups, and saucers. I arose in the morning, folded up the bed, retuning it into the couch crevice, reset the furniture, took a shower, and entered the living room to find the inspector reworking the layout and putting his final touches to the furniture's location.

Dad had the same furniture he and Mom had purchased after their honeymoon, each piece not for use but veneration. The living room couch, a relatively new purchase thirty-five years before, had a green Naugahyde cover "to protect the couch fabric." A clear plastic "to protect the Naugahyde" lay over it. And on top of the clear plastic cover lay an old white bed sheet "to avoid the plastic cover's uncomfortable effect on the body during cold and humid nights." The movers carried the couch down the two flights of stairs, turning abruptly right to enter the apartment. They set the couch in place on its respective tiles on the enlarged grid. That night as I pulled out the bed, I noticed a cut in the green Naugahyde, exposing a brown-orange fabric, the original fabric unseen for over thirty-five years.

In addition to layout design, Dad practiced general medicine. For the sake of our health, the window in the living room was never, ever to be open at night. This was New York City with summer temperatures of ninety degrees and humidity of ninety-five. No matter how hard I tried to keep the window open between one and six in the morning, Dad insisted on closing it. "The draft through an open window brings virus and disease, which you inhale while sleeping. Once entering your body, these villains enter your lungs. In your lungs, they combine with whatever is there and give you, God forbid, pneumonia. Now everyone knows pneumonia is bad, very bad; you can die from it. So shut the goddamn window."

Hot water training was also important in Dad's world. You never walked into the bathroom and turned on the hot water without first listening to the radiator and water pipes. If you heard water moving through the pipes, you had another cup of coffee. You never turned on the hot water or flushed, hearing water in the pipes. A flush could cause a significant aquatic hot flash that could be extremely painful. Dad's theory had some weaknesses. If you lived on a lower floor, you could not determine if anyone was using water since the pressure was greater and no one in the entire neighborhood listened that carefully. More often, I found the opposite problem—a frigid rush—impacting my water usage. I took many cold showers growing up on the top floor of our tenement although most of them started out as hot showers. Over the years, I learned the neighbor's schedules, arranging my shower schedule around theirs, both for their benefit and mine.

I normally scheduled my visits to New York in the spring, early summer, or fall, avoiding the extremes of the city's weather. One year the fall visit was set back until after Thanksgiving. I arrived at La Guardia ten at night on one of the last planes allowed to land in the heavy snowfall. Arriving at Dad's apartment at midnight, we shared news of family and friends in the kitchen, then pulled out the bed, and with window closed, of course, went to sleep.

Awaking early, I looked out the window to see heavy snow falling into the airshaft. Although I could not determine how much had accumulated on the ground, I immediately knew dinner at Porto Bello was not an option for Dad that night. After coffee and a piece or two of Entenmann's coffee cake, I explained to Dad I would go shopping and cook tonight's dinner. After several comments and weak protests, he acquiesced.

I stopped at the French meat market on Price Street between Sullivan and Thompson, where forty years ago Gumba Stanley's butcher shop had occupied the same location. I decided to make "Mom's Sunday Gravy" for Dad. Smiling despite my cold soaked feet, I placed my order for ground chuck, ground pork, Italian sausage, thinly sliced and pounded bottom chuck, together with a few pork spareribs, Dad's favorite.

On the corner of Prince and Thompson at M and O Groceries, I picked up the San Marzano tomatoes, tomato paste, eggs, breadcrumbs, Parmesan, and Locatelli, Romano cheese, mushrooms, onions, carrots, basil, garlic, and the most important ingredient, red wine. Walking across the street to Vesuvius Bakery, I chose an Italian loaf and some of my favorite hard baked bread with black pepper called *taralli*. On Sullivan Street, I began to walk toward Houston Street to purchase fresh mozzarella at Joe's Dairy. I abruptly stopped as the cold changed to freezing hail, turning back toward 120 Sullivan Street, deciding to modify the recipe using the available ingredients. The next day, a trip to Joe's Dairy wouldn't require a dog sled.

Hours later, I proudly served the meal to Dad. Sitting across from each other, starting with a long celebratory toast, we clinked glasses for good health. We finished dinner with sufficient leftovers remaining to ensure Dad several evenings of pasta after my visit ceased. I removed the plates from the table and began washing and drying, dishes, silverware, and pots and pans. I asked Dad, "So how was the meal?"

He quickly said, "Good, good, but a little too much sauce."

I laughed, "You haven't had a pot of sauce like this in over ten years—meatballs, sausage, pork, beef, and *braciole*—and you tell me too much sauce?"

He looked up, smiled, and said, "Well, it was good, but you were a little heavy-handed on the sauce."

We both laughed, I finished my wine, Dad his soda.

He got up to prepare for bed and said, "It's freezing, but if you want to leave the window open, it's OK."

Laughing we both went to bed, the window remained closed.

Six months later, Pat, the kids, and I called him on Easter Sunday morning to wish him a happy Easter. He asked, "How are you? Where are you going to spend the day?"

"We're going to have the Cavaliere's over for dinner and an Easter egg hunt. We'll be serving homemade *agnolotti* for twenty-five people."

Dad responded, "Remember, don't be too heavy with the sauce."

In New York, the snow melted the day after our home-cooked dinner. I told Dad, "I need to go to Macy's to buy some Christmas presents for the kids." He thought that was a good idea since he also wanted to get some new gloves. We caught a cab on Prince Street and Sixth Avenue and were at Thirty-fourth Street in twenty minutes. Entering Macy's, we headed for the back of the main floor to purchase his gloves then took the escalator up to Toyland. Toyland was busy, less than a month to go before Christmas; Dads, Moms, and children were everywhere. Confused, I looked around for a sign. I grabbed Dad's hand, walking him to the back of a long line of parents and young children.

Waiting in line, moving forward only inches after almost a half-hour, Dad said, "Why are we waiting on line to buy toys?"

"Macy's tries to make Christmas shopping for toys a pleasant experience, for children and parents. Limiting the number of people in the toy department provides better service and experiences for its shoppers," I replied.

Dad shook his head affirmatively, and we silently went back to our snail-like existence.

Another half-hour passed; we were now within eyesight of the front of the line. Dad's patience, of which he normally had an abundance, wore thin. "Let's go to another store."

"We're almost there, Dad. Hang in. We'll be at the head of the line in less than five minutes." Dad trusted my judgment since he was five foot two and could not see the front of the line.

A young woman dressed as a green elf gave me a card to fill out. Dad shook his head negatively, saying, "Filling out a card to get into

Toyland? These guys are going to go broke." We finally came to the head of the line! Dad could now see everything in front of him. "What are you nuts? You are really crazy. I ain't going to visit Santa Claus. I'm over eighty."

Laughing, I grabbed his hand, saying, "What have you got to lose? Santa is younger than either of us." The photograph of our visit with Santa is placed out every year with our Christmas decorations.

Our visits were special. Our time at the kitchen table and Porto Bello seemed more like two old friends who had not seen each other in a while getting together than father and son. Dinner during winter started earlier but still lasted several hours. Regardless of how engrossed Dad was in the conversation, he was always aware of his surroundings, something you learn in every big city.

At Porto Bello one evening, Al approached after dinner, knowing our dessert order before we spoke, decaffeinated coffee and a slice of cheesecake for Dad, an espresso and sambuca for me. This time Dad looked up, saying "No dessert; just the check."

"Are you OK?"

"I'm fine. I'll tell you on our way home after you pay the check."

Mind sprinting, brain filling with terrible negative thoughts, wearing a fake smile, I exited with Dad into the cold wet air of Thompson Street. "You OK?" I asked.

He nodded his head affirmatively. "I was looking at the door to the restaurant. There were six or eight people lined up, waiting for a table. It's winter; it's hard to fill a restaurant."

Two years later at our regular table for dinner, over coffee, I asked, "How are you doing?"

He paused, looked at me for a minute or so before responding, "It's getting hard to do all the things I need to do to live day by day."

Dad was now eighty-five; Aunt Rosie, all his friends, and his close support group were gone. The prostate cancer was affecting his strength and will. I held his hand, saying, "Are you ready to come out to Seattle, spend time with us, see your grandchildren?"

The answer never came in spoken words. Dad focused on the white tablecloth, picked up his teaspoon, held it in his hand, and dropped it onto the table as he nodded his consent.

I began arranging for Dad's move, consulting with him on every decision, knowing that for success to occur a significant buy-in was required. We said goodbye to family and friends at an early birthday party a few days before our departure. I was amazed at his strength, showing little emotion and preparing for a journey I know he did not want to make.

We spoke to his doctor who prescribed a mild sedative for Dad's first airplane ride. We packed the bags, gave him his sedative saying a teary goodbye to 120 Sullivan Street. At Kennedy, we entered the first-class section of a United DC-10, non-stop, a first for Dad and a first first-class flight for Pat and me.

Sitting next to Pat, Dad looked around. I was across the aisle. She described everything that would occur, attempting to smooth his anxieties. He listened now more intently since she had been correct on her previous forecasts. Pat arranged for doctors' appointments, medical records to be sent to Seattle, packing his luggage, and sending a portion of his apartment contents to his new home. Pat arranged visits for family members and friends to say goodbye. Dad was now a believer and trusted her.

Seated in first-class, we watched the remaining passengers enter the plane, passing us to reach their seats. Dad looked at each passenger, smiling and, for each pretty woman, extending the smile and tipping his pea cap in respect. The women smiled back, bowing their head in his direction. The flight attendants went through the first-class cabin, asking if anyone wanted a cocktail or wine. The flight attendant approached Dad, not realizing she was soon to confront a vast body of medical knowledge. Dad recounted his entire medical history, expressing his former belief in beer, now only in the power of ginger ale. Pat and I had a glass of red wine.

At cruising elevation, the seat belt sign turned off, and the flight attendants again made their way through the first-class cabin. "Would you like a refresher? Or something else?"

Dad looked up at the flight attendant. "I'd like some red wine."

Upon hearing the response, she put a glass of red wine on his serving tray. Pat and I both turned to Dad saying, "What?"

The flight attendant returned to the front of the cabin. Dad turned to Pat, gave her his wine glass, and said, "It's free. Let me know if you want more."

As we began, our approach to Sea-Tac, Pat told Dad about each sensation and sound he would experience on landing, the plane tilting when banking, aligning for the runway approach, the noise of lowering the landing gear, finally the bumps and contact with the runway, and the application of the brakes to slow down. We landed, and I watched my eighty-five-year-old father at the end of his first plane ride, a six-hour affair, smiling and looking in anticipation at whom he should tip his hat to. Our expectations exceeded, we wondered if we could get a copy of his prescription.

Waiting until the plane was almost empty before beginning our exit, Pat asked, "Dad were you comfortable?"

He smiled, saying, "I could do it again."

I grabbed his hand, pulling back the curtain between coach and first class, saying, "Good, but if you do decide to fly again, you'll sit back here." The three of us, laughing, holding hands, entered the terminal to meet the grandchildren.

We filled our time together in Seattle with laughter and happiness. Dad stayed at our house initially then, needing full-time care, moved to a nursing home a mile from our house, conveniently on the route I took to and from work. His strength in the beginning allowed us to take him to our house, always stopping at the local bakery. Assisted by his walker, he viewed the offerings in the display case with a smile as wide as the right and left supports of his walker, picking his strawberry shortcake or a cheesecake.

I visited him in the morning on my way to work, Pat and I again before or after dinner. We played gin, discussing our day, the grandchildren, and news of family. One evening, completing our third gin game, Pat indicated she was tired having had an early meeting that day, which would be repeated on the morrow. I recommended, "Let's throw in the hand. There're only five cards remaining. We can play tomorrow."

Dad met my eyes with a glassy stare. I smiled, asking him, "How many cards do you need for gin?"

"Only one."

I turned over the unplayed cards and exposed his hand. His gin card was one of the five unplayed cards. With a smile of disbelief, I asked my eighty-six-year old dad, in hospice and on pain medication, "Were you counting cards?" His laughter responded better than any words; he still "had it."

I left work early to visit Dad, arriving well before his dinner to speak to his hospice nurse about his medication and low blood count. After our discussion, I went to Dad's room. He was sitting up in bed, smiling. "Hey, how are you doing, kid?"

We sat across from each other and talked about our day. He looked down from my glance. I said, "You OK?"

He extended his hand. I immediately grasped it with both of mine. He said, "Good." His chin rested on his chest, his eyes closed. I held his hand in mine, tears streaming from my eyes in silence. It was then I knew I was now alone, no longer a child.

Hands

A baby's eyes uncovered,
Grasping at outstretched fingers.

Hands extended for support,
First steps, on stairs, crossing streets.

Hands avoided, growing up,
Asserting independence.

Hands joined in church,
Weddings, baptisms, funerals.

Hands grasped for support,
Doctor offices, emergency rooms.

Hands clasped to steady walks,
Climbing stairs, crossing streets.

Hands presented, eyes closed,
Saying goodbye.

Give me your hand.

We are a collage of the people we meet in our life's journey.

Thank you for allowing us to be a part of yours.

Rosemary and Big Mamma in front of 120 Sullivan Street

Epilogue

**Rosemary (Rosso) Muzio, D'avanzo
3 February 1938 – 20 November 2009**

Rosemary contributed to the stories, retrieved lost information, and provided descriptions and characterizations of our family and our neighborhood. My cousin made an indelible mark in the pages of this book, in the community in which we grew up, and upon the whole of my life. We are cousins and family soul mates, and her presence made my world a better place.

Rosemary voiced what I and most others in our neighborhood always believed:

Growing up in our neighborhood was one of the happiest times of my life.

About the Author

Tony Vivolo and his wife, Pat, have three children, Laura, Joe and Annemarie and three grand children Katherine, Michael and Zachary. Both retired, they now live on an island in the North Puget Sound of Washington State.